Live With It

Elise Moore was born and raised in Manitoba, goes to high school in Winnipeg, and aspires to write for *The Simpsons* one day. Elise Moore's other works include two short pieces, *Beverly Hills Waiting for Godot* and *Another Word for Bar*.

Live With It

Elise Moore

Blizzard Publishing • Winnipeg

Live With It first published 1994 by
Blizzard Publishing Inc.
301–89 Princess St., Winnipeg, Canada R3B 1K6
© 1994 Elise Moore

Cover photo: "Self-portrait" from *Self-portrait with Fish,
Pigs and Ballerinas, 1992,* by Marc "Hutch" Hutchison.

Printed in Canada by Kromar Printing Ltd.

Published with the assistance of
the Canada Council and the Manitoba Arts Council.

Caution

Canadian Cataloguing in Publication Data

Moore, Elise, 1975–
  Live with it
  A play.
  ISBN 0-921368-39-9
1. Orton, Joe, in literature. I. Title.
PS8576.067L5 1994   C812'.54   C94-920060-3
PR9199.3.M66L5 1994

"CHASUBLE: Your brother dead?

JACK: Quite dead.

MISS PRISM: What a lesson for him! I trust he will profit by it."

—Oscar Wilde
The Importance of Being Earnest

Live With It was first produced by Theatre Projects, Winnipeg, on February 22, 1994, with the following cast:

KEN	Richard Hurst
JOE	Ross McMillan

Directed by Rick Skene
Assistant Director: Ardith Boxall
Set and Costume Design by Rick Skene
Lighting Design by John J. Gilmore
Stage Manager: Carolyn Kutchyera

An earlier version of *Live With It* was first workshopped by Manitoba Association of Playwrights (MAP). The director was Yvette Nolan and the actors were Gene Pyrz, Richard Hurst and Richard Hirschfield. A subsequent MAP workshop was held in December, 1993, featuring the director and cast of the première production.

Playwright's Note

(The present. KEN and JOE are handcuffed together in Hell, sitting side by side on a bed.)

JOE: I wish I knew where the loo was.

KEN: Why? Contemplating cottaging in Hell? It's obvious death hasn't changed you one bit.

JOE: What'd you think, killing me would teach me a lesson? "Why thank you, Kenneth, due to your bashing my brains out I've come to appreciate the spiritual aspects of life and will now mend my ways and embrace society."

KEN: You'd shove it up the collective arse of the Celestial Host if so propositioned in a public lavatory.

JOE: It's only polite to accomodate one's host.

KEN: You'd have a foursome with the Holy Trinity.

JOE: How could I refuse three such reputable phallocentrics?

KEN: You're going to alienate the audience as usual.

JOE: *(Blithely.)* Oh, they'll sit here looking progressive and open-minded whilst I commit necrocide with their liberal ideals and afterwards they'll go home and discuss whether it was art or pornagraphy.

KEN: Would you kindly come down off your high horse a moment?

JOE: The way I feel right now I'd go down on my high horse. You could at least have informed me ahead of time—just a few crucial minutes—of the fate you had in store for me. Given the option of a final fuck—to repay me for allowing you to share the residual glory of my fame and fortune.

KEN: The only residue I saw was the kind collected on the inside of your underpants as I was washing them out in the sink. The only glory I was aware of was when you'd drop names as I was picking your socks up off the floor. A sensation almost as gratifying as editing your ever-abundant redundancies.

JOE: Then let me take this oppertunity to congratulate you on the fine job you did on my undergarments and manuscripts all those years. Except when you got them mixed up.

KEN: It was an honest mistake. They were both equally filthy.

JOE: And you, the man behind them both. Would you say you lived a full life, then, Ken? And you haven't even mentioned the occasional tug on my cock or valium tablet you kindly supplied me with.

KEN: *(Sententiously.)* The times, like underwear, must change. But not *you* ... you never change.

JOE: It's true I should've listened to my mum all those years ago: "Be sure to pack a sensible lunch and a change of underwear if you're going to be staying long in Hell."

KEN: I know there's no more pleasant way to pass an infernal eternity than insulting your audience's intelligence. Nevertheless, "liberal ideas" is an inexcusably archaic cliché.

JOE: A cliché, you say ... Wish I could remember what that was. Wait, it's coming back to me. Rather like ... bludgeoning?

KEN: *(Indicating the audience.)* They're desensitized to sex! Desensitized to *you! (Triumphantly.)* Now you finally know how I felt living with you all those years.

JOE: Cliché! Yes! Now it all comes back to me. *(To KEN.)* The world's smallest violin is playing just for you?

KEN: But to what avail? They're also desensitized to violins.

Elise Moore
February 1994

Characters

JOE: Joe Orton, the playwright
KEN: Kenneth Halliwell, his lover
(A boy)

Setting

London, England, August 9, 1967.

Act One

Scene One

(Spotlight on KEN's face in profile, bald-headed. He addresses the darkness in front of and just below him.)

KEN: Perpetual insomnia breeds strange nocturnal habits. *(Pause.)* A strange breed, we perpetual insomniacs. *(Pause. Musing.)* A self-perpetuating breed, we nocturnal strangers? *(Pause.)* Strangers in the night, exchanging venereal diseases ... *(Laughs. Pause.)* Watching the *play* of shadows on your face—memorizing each *line*. Not a few of which I've been at least partially responsible for, as you'd be the first to admit. This is my time for reflections. Not the kind confronted in polished surfaces, but in heads ... though in my case there's no need to make the distinction. I'd like to get inside your head and burrow in the breeding ground for polished wit and epigrams, a playground for the vernacular a verbatim, cheek at face value. Friends, Romans, countrymen ... lend me your rears. If only I could be certain I'm already in your dreams, I wouldn't have to use ... visual shock-tactics. If only the sound of your breathing in the darkness wasn't the only thing arguing I'm not alone.

(Pause. A sound of applause in the darkness. KEN looks around in bewilderment.)

JOE: *(From the surrounding darkness.)* How do you take your comedy?

KEN: *(Startled and confused.)* I beg your—

JOE: *(Interrupting.)* You were supposed to respond, "Black."

KEN: *(Still confused.)* I'm sorry.

JOE: *(Chiding.)* It's too late for apologies now. You've gone and spoilt the mood. Though that's not out of character for you. Let's shed some light, shall we? Then you can feel free to spill your guts on your sleeve to your heart's content.

KEN: *(Confused but angry.)* No! No light. I'm warning you ... *(Suddenly pleading.)* I'm *begging* you ... *(Recovers a bit.)* Why can't you leave me to my memories? I'm not disturbing anyone, you least of all. My memories of us are the only thing I have left that's mine alone, and then only by default. Because *you* don't want them.

> *(Lights come on suddenly. Their bedroom: two single beds, a bureau of sorts for clothing, shelves overflowing with books, a couple of chairs, also a telephone and record player. There is a desk with a typewriter. Also on the desk is JOE's journal, on top of which rests KEN's suicide note, surrounded by pills and a can of juice. There are two doors, one leading outside, one to the kitchen. KEN sits on a chair facing JOE's bed on which there is a sleeping figure representing Orton. KEN wears a pair of pyjamas; there is a hammer in his lap. JOE is in jeans and a white T-shirt. The time is 1967.)*

JOE: *(With camp sarcasm.)* You vant to be left alone? What you want if teaching those lines flattering to wearers of false eyelashes are not equally suited to wearers of false hair. However immortal the line may be, it's all in the delivery.

KEN: *(Still disoriented from the sudden light.)* Not one of your choicer cuts.

JOE: Actually, it's one of yours. You told it me years ago, during our days as struggling thespians.

KEN: You shouldn't've paid my banal bravado any mind. I couldn't act my way out of a prophylactic.

JOE: Your emotionally manipulative melodramatics make you sound like something out of a 40s "women's picture" featuring some darling of the queens like Crawford or Davis.

KEN: I'd need a cigarette for that. In fact, I need a cigarette.

> *(He pulls out a pack of cigarettes; lights one.)*

JOE: *(Coughing and grimacing.)* I wish you wouldn't smoke those foul things in our flat.

> *(KEN takes a long drag and exhales as he speaks, à la Bette Davis.)*

KEN: I wish you wouldn't fuck strange men in theirs. It's a matter of tit for tat.

JOE: Kindly keep your tits out of the discourse.

(JOE catches sight of something in KEN's lap: the hammer. He clearly sees it and reacts to it but decides not to say anything for the moment. KEN goes back to studying the sleeping figure.)

What do you find so captivating about watching me drool on my pillow? A wet-dream it's not. *(Peers over KEN's shoulder.)* The lines aren't really that obvious, are they? The lighting could be kinder. But all in all—

KEN: I didn't say—

JOE: Not bad at all. I'm still a young man. Young, good-looking, healthy, talented, famous, tolerably well-off and unequivocally well-hung. There's nothing in that bed to give rise to your self-indulgent theatrics. *(Pause. Then, suddenly.)* Ken? What's that in your lap?

(KEN gives JOE a withering look, then glances down. He's surprised but tries not to show it.)

KEN: It would appear to be a hammer.

JOE: *(Á la Lady Bracknell.)* A *handbag?!*

(Beat.)

(Didactic.) All pauses should be natural pauses. None of your long significant shit. Pace, pace, pace! Building up to the inevitable outcome. Everything the characters say is true. The rest is violence. *(Pause. In his normal voice.)* Why are you cradling that tool in your lap? *(Aside.)* We're assuming the hammer is real and not another illegitimate offspring of his deranged brain.

KEN: *(Annoyed.)* Of course it's real! What would I be doing with an imaginary hammer?

JOE: Back up a minute. We're still attempting to figure out what you'd be doing with a *real* hammer.

KEN: I know what I'm doing.

JOE: Do you?

KEN: Yes.

JOE: Then what?

(KEN stares at the hammer.)

KEN: I don't remember.

JOE: So we've ascertained that you still retain the capacity to distinguish between reality and fantasy. *(Pause. Prodding.)* Well? Haven't we?

KEN: *(Confused.)* I suppose so.

JOE: Suppose?

KEN: *(Ashamed.)* I've already forgotten.

JOE: *(Chiding.)* Forgotten already?

KEN: *(Exploding.)* I really don't see why all this is necessary!

JOE: Bear with me. *(Takes the hammer from KEN and holds it up.)* Using myself as an example of fantasy, and this appliance as an example of reality, you *can* distinguish between us, can't you?

KEN: *(With certainty.)* Yes.

JOE: Are you absolutely sure?

KEN: *(Less certain.)* Yes.

JOE: Can you trust what your senses perceive?

KEN: *(Not at all certain.)* Yes.

JOE: Good. That's important. Being able to rely on the infallibility of one's sensual perception is essential to one's peace of mind. Or pieces, if one is going to them.

KEN: *(Impatiently.)* And where is it you think you're going with this?

JOE: Way ahead of you. I just had to be convinced of your sweeping preeminence in the realm of reality. Now you can tell me what exactly you were planning to do with that hammer.

KEN: *(Wearily insolent.)* I told you. I don't know. Hang a picture, maybe?

   (JOE grabs him and shoves him to the floor.)

JOE: Wrong answer.

KEN: *(From the floor.)* I was acting under the assumption that the questions you've been posing are hypothetical, in which case there would be no right or wrong answers.

JOE: *(In KEN's face.)* I'm hypothetical. This *play* is. My questions are not. Answer them accordingly. *(Helps KEN up.)* Get a grip on reality.

   (JOE hands him the hammer; KEN flings it away violently.)

KEN: No!

JOE: *(Calmly retrieving it.)* Shut up. You'll wake me. Then where will you be?

   (JOE gently but firmly places the hammer in KEN's hand and holds it there.)

Let's assume you know what you're doing.

KEN: *(Warily.)* This is hypothetical?

JOE: What do you think?

KEN: You said *assume*. Therefore I'm *assuming* you meant to offer an hypothesis. Hypothetically, it could be that it's finally happened. I knew it was coming. I've experienced all the signs and symptoms.

JOE: You realize you're babbling.

KEN: *(With a kind of triumph.)* I've earned the right. I've lost my mind. Taken leave of my sense.

JOE: *(Scornfully.)* You're stalling.

KEN: I'm not—

JOE: And you can shove your excuses up your assumptions. Words, Ken, just words. Go on—it's your moment! Plead insanity all you please. But my sympathy has already been exhausted on sixteen years of trauma and trivia. All anticipating this. I like your suicidal style. My murder as accessory gives your pathetic end a touch of class. *(Picks up the note from the desk and reads.)* "If you read his diary all will be explained. K.H. ... P.S. Especially the latter part." *(Looks up at KEN.)* Very three-hanky. A hammer in hand, an ominous note and numerous Nembutals laid out meticulously on the desk.

KEN: Don't forget the grapefruit juice.

JOE: *(Sarcastically.)* And a can of grapefruit juice. Shall I also read the label?

　　(Pause.)

　　(Exploding.) Pace, pace, pace! If you're going to do me in, do it now. It's what I'd do in your place.

KEN: Whose side are you on?

JOE: Ask yourself that.

KEN: You think I haven't?

JOE: What do I know about what you think?

KEN: You know me.

JOE: Is that what you think?

KEN: Answer me!

JOE: Tutu, Brutus?

KEN: *(Enraged.)* Words, bleeding words!

JOE: *(Without expression.)* Pace.

KEN: I'm in pain!

JOE: Pace.

KEN: Pain!

JOE: Pace.

> *(Pause.)*

KEN: Pause.

> *(With a cry of rage KEN swings at JOE with the hammer. JOE catches KEN's arm and then, producing a pair of handcuffs, previously concealed, he handcuffs himself to KEN. JOE tries to force the hammer, which KEN is still clutching, down on the sleeping figure's head.)*

No!

JOE: Wrong answer.

KEN: I *can't—*

JOE: Haven't you heard? The queen is mightier than the sword.

KEN: *(Pleading.)* Joe—?

JOE: Everything the characters say is true.

KEN: Please.

JOE: And you say—

KEN: Don't, Joe, *please,* I can't—

JOE: Wrong answer. From the top. And you say—

KEN: *(Quietly, desperately.)* Black.

JOE: Again. Louder. And you say—

KEN: Black!

> *(KEN is losing the struggle; the hammer is going down.)*

JOE: And you say—

> *(JOE abruptly loses interest and heads for his leather cap, resting on a chair; KEN, still handcuffed, is dragged after him.)*

KEN: Where are you going?

JOE: For a walk.

> *(JOE puts on his cap; KEN drops the hammer. Lighting change. JOE drags KEN to an empty area of the stage. A spotlight follows them. Throughout the following JOE appears to be unaware of*

KEN's presence. JOE eyes "The Boy," who can be played by a third actor or by KEN speaking his lines. KEN addresses his next comments to the audience.)

KEN: This is Joe Orton on the prowl. Observe the strut: pelvis and lower lip out; obligatory rakish tilt to cap.

JOE and KEN: *(KEN mockingly.)* Smashing.

KEN: He'd pick himself up if he could.

(KEN looks in the direction JOE is peering in.)

The English urban fairy ogling a potential pick-up: the over-sexed in full pursuit of the under-aged. They eye each other up warily. "Not bad." But don't look too anxious. "Is he or isn't he? Is he a cop?" Look around furtively. No one in sight. Fortune smiles on our trifles. How do I know all this? Do you imagine I partake in this sordid, squalid, socially stigmatized ritual? No. But he returns following each foray with the bloody anecdote, still dripping viscera, falling from his mouth as he stalks through the door. And I sit there looking blasé, trying to think up caustic comments which he'll include in his account of the encounter when he writes it up in his diary. The posteriors of every other anonymous queen in London, preserved for posterity. Including my own—in its supporting role.

JOE: Hey.

KEN: Here it comes.

BOY: Yer?

KEN: And here we go.

JOE: Got a name?

BOY: No.

JOE: My name's Kenneth.

KEN: Oh, lovely!

BOY: That's a nice name. Look, I have to—

KEN: But he won't.

BOY: I don't want to—

KEN: But he will.

JOE: Do you kiss?

BOY: No.

KEN: Yes—

JOE: Take it?

BOY: No!

KEN: Yes—

JOE: Got a place?

BOY: No.

KEN: Yes—

JOE: See I'm handcuffed to someone at the moment which makes it awkward—

KEN: *(In a rage.)* Yes, yes, yes!!!

JOE: No one's about ...

BOY: No ...

KEN: *(To JOE.)* What am I then? An unsightly growth on your wrist? A figment of your depraved imagination?

> *(JOE mimes backing "the boy" into a doorstep, glances around; KEN is dragged along.)*

Oh, lovely. A doorstep in broad daylight. This is really taking the concept of public sex a step too far.

JOE: How old are you?

BOY: Seventeen.

KEN: Jailbait, Joe. Of course so were you when we started living together. Nevertheless I never took you in the open air in a public square like this.

JOE: I like them about fourteen.

BOY: Sorry.

JOE: Don't apologize.

BOY: Kenneth—

JOE and KEN: Yes?

BOY: What are you going to do with me?

JOE: Well first I'm going to fuck you very quickly and thoroughly.

BOY: No, *please.*

JOE: Shut up. I'm going to fuck you now.

KEN: *(To audience.)* Seen enough?

> *(JOE and the boy freeze in their positions.)*

Now I finally have you where you can't get away or talk over me. Now I'm going to tell you what I think for once. I don't mind this. I mean, there's nothing I can do about it. What I mean is, I could live with this. Only, of course, I can't follow you about all the time and keep an eye on you—except in my mind's eye. Instead I sit with my thumb up my arse staring at the ceiling of our cozy clausterphobic closet, our exclusive cramped cell. Hugged and hemmed in by the four oppressive walls, held snugly in place, nursing kinks. But what did you expect? Pouring your poisonous repertoire in my ears at all hours ... *What do you expect?* Do you keep me around as your conscience, or as your warden? Or as your prisoner? Who am I kidding? I'm just your glorified housemaid.

(Blackout.)

Scene Two

(A kettle screams in the darkness. Lights up on the bedroom. JOE and KEN, free of handcuffs, sit on their separate beds. It is 1967.)

JOE: So all the while I fucked him up against the wall he kept shouting for me to stop. He was loud enough I was afraid someone would come running and discover us there. Some unsuspecting passing pedestrian. In fact a few individuals answering to that description did happen by and I had to pull out and pull up my jeans and give him my fist to suck on to keep him quiet. *(Grins at the memory.)* We must have looked a sight.

KEN: *(Getting up.)* I hear the kettle. *(As he goes towards the kitchen.)* He wasn't serious about wanting you to stop.

JOE: *(Calling to kitchen.)* Oh, no. I thought at first he might be, you see. But then I realized it was part of his obligatory kink. Afterwards he even thanked me for continuing. "How did you know exactly what I needed, Kenneth?"

(KEN re-enters with teapot, cups, etc., on a tray.)

KEN: "Kenneth"—?

JOE: I told him my name was Kenneth.

KEN: *(Pouring the tea.)* I wonder what my psychiatrist would say about that.

JOE: "What I really needed was a good fucking," he said. "Where did you learn to fuck like that? I haven't had such a good *(Mispronouncing.)* fuching—"

KEN: "Such a good *fucking*." Sugar?

JOE: Thank you, and please. "I haven't had such a fucking in ages."

>   *(KEN hands JOE his tea; JOE takes a sip.)*

>   I told him we must fuck again sometime.

KEN: So if anyone calls wanting to fuck with Kenneth, I'll know it's not for me.

JOE: *(Indicating the tea.)* It wants more sugar. I didn't give him our number.

KEN: I must've given you mine by mistake.

>   *(They trade teacups, then sit sipping for a moment on their separate beds.)*

>   Why don't you tell them your real name.

JOE: "Them"?

KEN: Your pick-ups.

JOE: I prefer my public and private lives not become gratuitously entangled. If they're relatively at ease, their dialogue is natural. Hence I get to observe the average working Joe in his natural habitat, and the sex is hotter into the bargain. Were they aware I'm a playwright of some repute, unnecessary complications could arise. The general public doesn't seem to understand that playwrights fuck and have shits and pick their noses. Just like you mere mortals.

KEN: I doubt any of them have heard of you anyway. You hardly pick and choose on the basis of cerebral endowments.

JOE: There's always the off-chance, now I've had my picture in the papers. Just the other day I had someone say to me on the bus, "Aren't you Joe Orton?" It's the first time I've been recognized.

KEN: Really? Just the other day I had someone on the bus say to me, "Get out of the way, arsehole, are you blind or just a moron?" *(Pause. Sips.)* How's your tea?

JOE: A little weak.

KEN: More sugar?

JOE: Have you any valium?

KEN: Tea and valium. How decadent.

>   *(He fetches a bottle from a drawer of the desk. They both take a couple each.)*

JOE: *(Yawning.)* I ought to be getting to bed soon. Have to spend tomorrow typing. *(Pulling off his jeans.)* Wonder what the *Daily Telegraph* will say to this one?

KEN: "Orton Opens His Fly in the Face of Convention."

> *(They laugh. JOE moves to get ready for bed.)*

I don't suppose you feel like having sex.

JOE: Why? Did my take excite your fancy?

KEN: *(Defensive.)* Nothing like that. It was merely a question.

JOE: In that case, not really.

KEN: Not really what?

JOE: I don't much feel like having it, no.

KEN: I see. Goodnight, then.

> *(KEN turns down the covers and prepares to climb into bed.)*

JOE: But if you want to I'm willing.

> *(Pause. KEN considers this. Then he sits on the bed beside JOE and allows JOE to undress him.)*

KEN: There's no point anyway. You'll just get me pleasantly aroused and then not be able to fuck me.

JOE: *(Pulling down KEN's bottoms.)* It's not some kind of elaborate plot on my part to make you feel even more inadequate than you already do.

KEN: So you constantly claim.

JOE: *(Half-jokingly.)* Perhaps I can never fuck you because I'm stopped by my reflection in your eyes. Did you ever think of that, Ken?

KEN: That's very poetic. I could always close them.

JOE: That wouldn't make any difference. I'd still be able to see myself reflected in your head.

KEN: You epic-length prick.

> *(They make out on the bed. It should be equally passionate and comical. KEN struggles to keep his wig on.)*

JOE: This is amazing.

KEN: Thank you.

JOE: I meant the valium.

KEN: I know.

(Their passion increases and KEN's wig falls off. He sits up to retrieve it.)

(Replacing his wig.) You had to toss that in, didn't you?

JOE: What?

KEN: "I don't feel much like having sex."

JOE: I've changed my mind. I'm being fickle and unpredictable. Just pretend my spontaneity arouses you.

(JOE tries to kiss KEN, who is angry and looking slightly ludicrous in his boxer shorts with his wig askew. KEN resists.)

KEN: You're simply incapable of being in any way intimate with me without first making sure I realize you're doing me a favour.

JOE: *(Also becoming angry.)* As I look at it, I am. I'm tired. I've had my sex for the evening. I wasn't interested in extending my library ticket—

KEN: Pity.

JOE: What is?

KEN: You keep me around because you pity me. Don't you.

JOE: You're right, Ken, all right? Your astounding ability to unravel the complexities of human nature has triumphed as usual. I've stayed with you these sixteen years out of sheer pity just because I'm such a sensitive and caring human being.

KEN: You make a mockery of everything!

JOE: Don't fob your prefab paranoia off on me. I'm sorry it offends your fading Southern self-esteem that I can't fuck you. Perhaps your psychiatrist could explain it to you. I can't.

KEN: This is not about sex! It's about your not touching me, or looking at me, or listening to me—

JOE: I can't listen to this. I'm tired. I just want to go to bed. *(Pause.)* When I touch you lately you push me away or make excuses.

KEN: Because I know you really don't want to.

JOE: Silly me, I should've been more explicit. After all, I'm always forcing myself to do that which is repulsive to me. It has to do with the deep and intense guilt that plagues me concerning my homosexual activities.

KEN: You go out and find some faceless boy to fuck!

JOE: Exactly: faceless! Just a prick and some perfunctory dialogue. We wouldn't have to go through this again and again if you could somehow allow yourself to believe you might actually be more to me than—

KEN: A glorified housemaid?

JOE: *(After a disgusted pause.)* I hear Hell is nice this time of year. The social season is in full swing. Perhaps you'd care to peruse a brochure. As for me, I'm going to sleep.

(JOE reaches over and turns out the light.)

KEN: *(In the darkness.)* I'm not going anywhere without you.

Scene Three

(Music: "She's Leaving Home." Lights fade up on the kitchen. KEN, in his wig, is sitting at the table, peering into a compact and applying some rouge. The door leading outside is heard opening and slamming shut. KEN pretends not to notice. JOE comes in wearing his jacket and cap, which he removes.)

JOE: Trying for a more life-like appearance? Were I you I'd opt for professional help.

KEN: A makeover? I don't think I've disintegrated to the decadent standards of Professor Aschnbach during his dolorous last days, do you?

JOE: I meant a mortician.

(Pause. JOE gets a bottle of milk from the fridge and a glass from the cupboard. He sits at the table and pours himself a glass. KEN puts away the compact. The music has faded completely away.)

KEN: So where were you?

JOE: Walking.

KEN: Walking where?

JOE: Walking around, up, down, in , out, about, through, by, under, over, all over. Walking. It's not one of my more insidious vices.

(He gulps the milk and pours himself another glass, which he sips at.)

KEN: You're late.

JOE: I was held up.

KEN: How? By what? Or should I be asking by whom?

JOE: Why do you care? I'm here, aren't I?

KEN: You have no consideration. None. To a person with any consideration to speak of the reason for my concern would be obvious. But as
I'm talking to you I see I'll have to elaborate. You tell me you'll be
home by a certain hour; I expect you home by a certain hour. When
you don't show up, I get worried. Why do I care, indeed.

JOE: *(Casually.)* Yes, sorry. You wouldn't happen to've made dinner? I
thought I smelled something when I came in.

KEN: *(Exploding.)* You're fucking right something smells! I made your
dinner! I timed it to be ready twenty minutes ago! It's cold now! It's
cold because you're twenty fucking minutes late!

JOE: *(Quietly, calmly.)* Thank you for making me dinner. I'm sorry it's
cold but we could warm it up in the oven.

KEN: We wouldn't have to warm it up if you'd been on time in the
first place!

JOE: I'll warm it up. Do you want me to warm it up?

KEN: What do you know about it?

JOE: I'm perfectly capable of preparing my own meals, Kenneth. I don't
need you to cater to me like some glorified housemaid.

KEN: You'd be fucking nothing without me!

JOE: *(Shouting back now.)* What does that have to do with dinner?
Nothing, that's what!

KEN: Everything! Everything. It has to do with respect. And the fact that
I'm not—

(He catches himself and stops.)

JOE: What? *(Mocking.)* "Getting any"?

KEN: *(Not backing down.)* That's exactly the sort of third-rate rot
that would've kept you buried in obscurity were I not around to
edit you.

JOE: *(Trying to regain control.)* How's this one then: Before this goes
any further, why don't we eat our meal in peace like what I hesitantly
call "normal people" do.

KEN: Fuck normal people!

*(JOE rushes towards KEN, looking about to belt him. Instead he
grabs his jacket from the table where he dumped it and heads for
the door.)*

Fine. Run away. That's all your good for anymore. Run headlong into the wide-flung arms of your worshipful minions. You think it won't matter if you're a few minutes late. You actually expect me to compete for your attention with those slobbering, sycophantic court hermaphrodites who worship the ground you piss upon. *(Contemptuously.) John Kingsley Orton.* Does that name sound familiar to you? Why should it? No one's ever heard of it. No one who's anyone. You want some reminding of your humble beginnings.

(JOE collapses in a chair, exhausted.)

JOE: I couldn't possible forget. Not with you around.

KEN: *(Screaming.)* You're fucking right!

JOE: Stop screaming.

KEN: Does this sound like screaming to you?

JOE: Yes, actually.

KEN: Do you want to know why I'm screaming?

JOE: Actually—

KEN: *(Starting to cry.)* Because it's the only way I can get you to hear me. Joe, you've got to have some consideration for me.

JOE: *(Mumbling wearily, with his eyes closed.)* I'm sorry. I'll try harder next time.

KEN: But it hurts *now.*

JOE: I'm sorry.

KEN: Most of the time you don't act like you notice I'm here.

JOE: Sorry.

KEN: *(Screaming.)* You're not listening to me!

JOE: *(Opening his eyes and standing.)* I've got a fucking headache, okay?

(He goes to the cupboards and starts searching through them.)

Where did you hide the valium?

KEN: I ought to hide them, at the rate you're going through them.

(JOE finds the pills, takes a couple and offers the bottle to KEN, who shakes his head. KEN pulls out a cigarette and lights it.)

JOE: What'd I tell you about that?

KEN: You're using up all my valium. You, the *raison d'être* for my dependency. I need something to soothe my nerves. *(Pause as KEN puffs.)* When's the last time we had sex?

JOE: What?

KEN: Sex, Joe. Fucking. We used to do that occasionally.

JOE: If you want to call it that.

KEN: Oh, pardon me. I realize your experience in the realm of *fucking* is far wider and varied than my own. What's the word for what we used to do, and don't do anymore? Help me out. You're the playwright.

> *(JOE goes over to KEN, gently takes the cigarette from his fingers and sets it in an ashtray.)*

You never touch me anymore.

> *(JOE touches KEN's shoulder.)*

JOE: *(Meaning it this time.)* I'm sorry.

KEN: You don't treat me like I'm alive.

JOE: *(Very softly.)* That's because you don't act like it.

KEN: *(Same.)* That's because you don't treat me like it.

JOE: That's because you don't act like it.

KEN: That's because—

> *(JOE kisses him on the lips and presses his body close. It's a very long kiss. JOE moves his hand to KEN's crotch; KEN abruptly shoves the hand away and breaks away from the embrace. He resumes his cigarette.)*

Your dinner's congealing.

JOE: *(Disgusted.)* I don't believe you.

KEN: I'm only thinking of you.

JOE: I'm going out.

KEN: Where?

JOE: For a walk.

KEN: For a walk *where?*

JOE: Don't wait up for me.

> *(He starts to go.)*

KEN: Joe.

JOE: What?!

KEN: I'm sorry. Stay home tonight. For once. For me. I didn't mean to shove you away. It's just my nerves. And my health in general. I'm in a bad state. But I'm seeing a new doctor. Did I tell you? And I've an appointment with a new psychiatrist. I'm going to get better. *(Giggles nervously.)* My former psychiatrist said I feel guilty about my mother's death and that's the root of all my problems.

JOE: What on earth do you have to feel guilty about? There was nothing you could do.

KEN: I'm just telling you what he said. Are you staying? I'll make tea. We can … talk.

JOE: There's nothing left to talk about. Nothing left but to claw at the carcass of our former conversations. And I'm sick of it. I'm sick of death. I want to go for a walk.

KEN: Please, Joe.

JOE: *(Knowing he won't.)* You can come with me if you like.

KEN: You're going to pick someone up. Is that it?

JOE: *(Satirically.)* It'd give us something to chat about over tea.

KEN: *(Going into another rage.)* Well you're not to bring him back here. I'll not have you bringing rough trade up to the flat.

JOE: I don't pick up "rough trade," Kenneth. I've never had trouble with a boy in my life.

KEN: Well there's always a first time and I'll not have it happen here. I'll not have it, do you hear me? Anyway, who wants your trash cluttering up the room. And who wants you? You trash. I work at cleaning this place for you all day from top to fucking bottom and what do you do? You want to bring the garbage home and fuck it on the bed. *I'll not have it!*

(JOE has put on his jacket and cap and is heading for the door.)

Joe? Don't you want some dinner before you go? It won't take me long to heat up. You can heat it up if you like.

JOE: *(Pausing by the doorway.)* No thanks. I'm not really hungry. *(Pause.)* You're sure you don't want to come.

KEN: No, thank you. No sense letting a good meal go to waste. I'll save you the leftovers. In a container in the refrigerator.

JOE: Thanks. I probably won't be in till late. I'll try not to wake you when I get in.

KEN: I'll probably be up. I don't sleep much lately.

(Pause.)

JOE: I'm off then.

(KEN doesn't respond. JOE turns to go, then pauses and turns back.)

You've nothing to feel guilty about. Sleep on that.

(Blackout. Pause. The outer door slams.)

Scene Four

(The Royal Academy of Dramatic Art, 1951. An empty area of the stage. KEN enters dressed theatrically: a black pin-stripe suit, black tie, black beret—no wig, and a camel-hair overcoat with a sash belt. He walks a few steps, a spotlight following him, then suddenly stops and dramatically flings his coat into a corner. His expression is inscrutable. He begins to mime petting a cat, cuddling and stroking it lovingly. Suddenly his expression changes. He becomes enraged and violently strangles the imaginary animal. He holds the limp body for a moment, and then his expression once again becomes inscrutable. He takes his bows, then walks away. JOE enters and sits where KEN was last, cross-legged on the floor, reading a book. He wears nondescript trousers and a shirt. KEN re-enters, looks at JOE, looks around uncertainly.)

KEN: *(Calls to JOE.)* Excuse me.

(JOE looks up in surprise, looks around.)

Yes, you. Have you perchance seen a coat lying about here?

JOE: Coat?

(JOE's responses are very nervous and faltering, his working class accent more noticeable here than in other scenes.)

KEN: It's difficult to miss. Genuine camel-hair, you know.

JOE: *(Glances around.)* Is that it over there?

(KEN goes to fetch his coat.)

KEN: Thank god. I was afraid someone might've made off with it.

JOE: I was tempted. It looks very suptuous. *(Repeating the word in the hope that KEN won't notice he made a mistake the first time.)* That's exactly the word to describe it. *Sumptuous.*

KEN: *(Flinging the coat over his shoulder flamboyantly.)* Not really. Just one of my little affectations. I like to indulge myself occasionally.

JOE: That's a healthy attitude.

(Pause. JOE self-consciously goes back to reading his book. KEN pulls a handkerchief from the pocket of his overcoat, wipes his

hands, dabs at his forehead, then strides towards JOE with a sense of purpose.)

KEN: What is it you're reading.

JOE: Shakespeare.

KEN: I see. *(Quoting dramatically.)*

"My glass shall not persuade me I am old,
So long as youth and thou are of one date,
But when in thee Time's furrows I behold,
Then look I death my days should expiate.
For all the beauty that doth cover thee
Is but a seemly raiment of my heart,
Which in thy breast doth live, as thine in me.
How can I then be elder than thou art?"

(Pause. He clears his throat.)

That's from the Sonnets.

(Pause.)

JOE: That was very nice.

KEN: Which play are you reading? *(Quickly.)* Let me guess. *King Lear*?

JOE: *The Tempest.* I'm reading it for Ariel. It's my favourite part in all of Shakespeare.

KEN: So this isn't your first foray into the world of the immortal bard. Very impressive. Though I prefer Marlowe, myself. Given the choice, I'd rather have been a king's favourite than a queen. You?

JOE: *(Not having understood a word.)* I played Ariel once.

KEN: For a production, or for class? Either way, I regret to've missed it. You'd make an exceptional Ariel.

JOE: D'you think so?

KEN: Quite. You know, of course, that all of Shakespeare's female roles were originally written for boy actors.

JOE: *(He did.)* Of course.

KEN: Ariel must be interpreted by a male. There is no other way the part can be properly played.

JOE: That's what I think, also. But when I said I'd played Ariel, I'm afraid I only meant I read a speech for my elocution teacher, Madame Rothery. *(Trying desperately to appear sophisticated.)* Perhaps you've heard of her?

KEN: I don't believe so.

JOE: Well, it doesn't matter now, I got rid of the bitch as soon as I was accepted into the Academy. *(Bashfully.)* Sorry about the language.

KEN: What do you mean? A cunt by any other name would be as smelly a spectacle.

JOE: You're very different from my mum, you know.

KEN: I should hope so.

JOE: She can cuss like a sailor when something gets her dander up, but if she ever caught me following suit she'd threaten to wallop me one. She can do it, too.

KEN: What was your quarrel with this "Madame Rothery"?

JOE: She told me I sound gutter. That's why I was taking the lessons, see. To learn to sound more sophisticated, and refined. I didn't mind her saying so. Much. But the cunt *(Glances at KEN for approval.)* didn't think I could learn any better. Not that I've done much to prove her wrong. Yet.

KEN: I think your accent is charming. It sets you apart.

JOE: You think so?

KEN: That and your looks.

   (Embarrassed pause.)

What "gutter" is it you hail from?

JOE: *(With a grimace.)* Leicester. My dad's a gardener. He's almost blind.

KEN: And your blaspheming mother?

JOE: She doesn't work anymore. Her eyes are bad too. Used to be she worked at a sewing machine—in a factory. It's what did her eyes in. Now she's a char. *(Pause.)* It wasn't a gutter so much as a well of boredom. Though Mum likes to pretend like we're lapping up luxury left and right. D'you know she once got herself up in gold lamé just to go around the corner? Even painted her shoes gold. The paint cracked when she walked and she left a trail of gold dust stretching from our front door on into the pub.

KEN: *(Laughing.)* No!

JOE: *(Same.)* Yes!

KEN: *(Slowly; making a pronouncement.)* I'll bet she hates fucking.

JOE: *(Eyes wide.)* What?

KEN: Sex. You know. Fucking.

JOE: D'you know you're right. That's what she's always saying. "How I ever got four children I'll never know. It were pure hell!" *(Pause.)* So what're your parents. Something real high-class and respected, I'll bet.

KEN: My parents are dead.

JOE: *(Taking this in stride.)* We should all be so blessed. Sorry if I sound in poor taste but I guess you start expecting these things to happen when you reach your age.

KEN: I'm twenty-five.

JOE: *(Shocked.)* I thought you were a lot older than that. *(Catching himself.)* I mean you come off so much more distinguished than most of the other students. *(Pause.)* Most of them are afraid of you, Mr. Halliwell.

KEN: You may call me Kenneth. *(Suddenly realizing.)* How did you know my name?

JOE: *(Sheepishly.)* I noticed you in class. You're difficult to miss. I saw your mime in class this morning, with the cat.

KEN: What did you think of it?

JOE: *(Genuinely enthusiastic.)* Think of it? I loved it! *(Catches himself.)* That is, I thought it was ... most effective. *(Pause.)* I'll bet you have no idea who I am.

KEN: That's not true. You're Joe.

JOE: John.

KEN: Yes, of course.

JOE: John Orton.

(They shake hands awkwardly. Pause.)

KEN: You said the other students are ... "afraid" of me?

JOE: Intimidated, I guess I mean.

KEN: How do you know this?

JOE: I know because they tell me. They treat me like I'm one of them. Because I make them laugh, I guess. I pretend to be friendly so they won't treat me badly on account of my accent. But I'm not—one of them. They can be so snobby and stand-offish, so ...

KEN: Pretentious?

JOE: Yeah, exactly. Always pretending like they're fountains of knowledge, always spouting off ...

KEN: It's only to be expected, John. You know what happens when idle hands get hold of a little learning.

JOE: Yeah. They're afraid of anyone who's different from average.

KEN: Or better than the same.

JOE: Like you.

KEN: And like you.

JOE: Yeah. *(Pause.)* I'm sorry.

KEN: For?

JOE: Your parents—what I said.

KEN: That's all right. You didn't realize.

JOE: That's no excuse. Anyway, I didn't mean it like it sounded.

KEN: It's all right. My mother's been dead some time. And it wasn't difficult to adjust to my father's absence, as we never did make a habit of acknowledging each other's existence.

JOE: What happened to them? Was it an accident?

KEN: *(Sententiously.)* Dwelling on the morbid past is a mark of regression.

JOE: Sorry.

KEN: Don't apologize.

> *(Pause.)*

JOE: I bet you don't find me so bleeding charming now.

KEN: Certainly I do. In fact, I predict your charm will be a great asset to you in life. Lord knows I could use some.

JOE: But it's like I said, you're so distinguished, you don't need charm. *(Pause.)* That's not what I meant. *(Burning with embarrassment, he grabs his book and turns to go.)* I'd better be off.

KEN: John, wait.

> *(Impulsively, he grasps JOE's shoulders and turns JOE to face him.)*

JOE: *(Miserably.)* What do you want?

> *(KEN takes the book from him and tosses it on the floor, the takes JOE's hands and looks straight at him.)*

KEN: It's all right.

> *(Pause. They look at each other. Then KEN nervously steps back, pulling out his handkerchief to wipe his hands.)*

JOE: *(Remaining close to KEN.)* That really is a lovely coat. *(Pause.)* May I stroke your camel-fur?

KEN: *(Not looking at him.)* What? No!

> *(Pause. KEN takes off the coat and hands it to JOE.)*

> Here. You can have it.

JOE: *(Surprised and excited.)* I couldn't!

KEN: *(Almost angrily.)* Of course you can! Take it.

> *(Pause. JOE is staring at KEN. He comes to a quick decision.)*

JOE: *(Turning around and holding out his arms.)* Will you help me with it on?

KEN: *(Obliging grudgingly.)* I hardly think this is necessary. I'm sure you're capable of dressing yourself.

JOE: Four arms are better than two.

KEN: And foreskins are the most fun of all.

JOE: *(Turns to face KEN.)* What d'you think?

KEN: Sumptuous. Exactly the word to describe it.

JOE: So we're friends now.

KEN: That depends. Are *you* intimidated by me, John?

JOE: Never was. I thought you were mysterious and distinguished. Not dangerous.

KEN: Don't be so sure.

> *(JOE struts across the stage, chin up, nose in the air.)*

> Just what do you think you're doing?

JOE: *(Good-humouredly imitating KEN's didactic, prissy tone.)* I'm Kenneth Halliwell. I'm *dangerous. (Walks boldly up to KEN.)* To complete the effect.

> *(He reaches to grab KEN's beret from his head.)*

KEN: *(Sharply.)* John!

> *(KEN reflexively slaps him. They are both shocked by the action. JOE stares at KEN a moment. Then he turns and hurriedly picks up his book.)*

> *(Blurts it out.)* Let me buy you a drink.

JOE: *(Astonished.)* Alcohol?

KEN: Yes. *(With some of his former affectation.)* I'm of age.

JOE: I don't drink.

KEN: You could make an exception.

JOE: Why should I?

KEN: Because it's the least I can do.

> *(Pause. JOE considers this.)*

JOE: That's true. *(Pause.)* You could buy me a coke.

KEN: *(Relieved.)* My pleasure.

JOE: Then let's go.

> *(JOE walks off, ignoring KEN, who hurries after him. Blackout.)*

Scene Five

> *(Several months later. KEN's flat: a double-bed; books everywhere; a desk and a typewriter. KEN sits on the bed with JOE, who is reading, in his lap. KEN is stroking JOE's hair.)*

KEN: My pussycat.

JOE: Piss off, Ken, I'm reading.

KEN: I don't love you for your mind.

JOE: I thought you were trying to educate it.

KEN: There's more to life than books.

JOE: *(Hands KEN a book.)* Here. Stimulate your intellect. Or wank yourself off with it for all I care. Only leave me read in peace. You're drooling all over the *Symposium*.

> *(KEN throws the book across the room. JOE ignores this and continues reading. KEN yanks the book out of JOE's hands and throws it after the other one. JOE sits perfectly still for a minute, then gets up to get it. KEN grabs him and spins him around.)*

KEN: I don't think you're even a proper homosexual.

JOE: *(Shakes off KEN's hand.)* That's not worth a response.

> *(He sits back down with his book.)*

KEN: I'll add that to my list of things you don't respond to. *(Pause.)* It's me, isn't it? Something I've done. Or something I could be doing I'm not.

JOE: The area of my personal fetishes is a murky one. I'd advise you to keep out of it if you want to retain any respect for me as a fellow civilized human being.

KEN: You've never pretended to be civilized. It's one of the things that attracted me to you in the first place.

(Pause.)

JOE: Sometimes ... I don't appreciate the way you treat me.

KEN: What way is that.

JOE: Like I'm some kind of glorified ... office-boy ... geisha girl ...

KEN: A titillating amalgam. Go on.

JOE: *(Becoming agitated.)* Like any time you want to use me for sex or to run your errands or endure another of your dramatic recitations I should automatically be ready as though I had nothing better to do than accommodate your least whim.

KEN: I'm working and looking towards the future. I'm thinking of you, too, you know. What're you contributing?

JOE: All I can! That's why I was sitting here reading a fucking book when I could be out pursuing more common, callow youthful activities. Like having fun.

KEN: And I'm no fun at all, am I?

JOE: You're bloody right you're not!

KEN: You're talking like a shop-assistant again.

JOE: *(Sulking.)* What do you care how I talk? You don't love me for my mind.

KEN: Don't be childish.

JOE: It's how you treat me. Carrying on half the time like we're destined for glory.

KEN: That's only on the rare occasion I can make myself heard over your bitching.

JOE: I wish on one such occasion you'd take advantage of the opportunity to explain how we're going to become famous actors playing walk-on parts in gloomy repertory theatres that no one ever attends because they're damp and cold and the plays are dead shitty. But there it is. What else can I do besides act—*type?*

KEN: *(Indicating his desk.)* Look in the second drawer on the far right.

(JOE looks hesitant.)

Do it, John.

JOE: *(Retrieving a manuscript.)* What's this?

KEN: My novel.

JOE: *(In disbelief and awe.)* All this?

KEN: One day when I'm the published recipient of critical accolades, you'll be proud to've known Kenneth Halliwell.

JOE: *(Sits on KEN's knee.)* I already am.

(They kiss.)

KEN: You could be of great help to me, you know.

JOE: *(Playfully.)* As your inspiration?

KEN: I meant you could put your skills, such as they are, to good use typing my manuscripts.

(KEN is unbuttoning JOE's shirt. He doesn't notice that JOE is no longer responding until JOE pushes him away, gets up and buttons his shirt.)

JOE: I guess I'd better get started.

KEN: Started?

JOE: *(Sits at desk.)* On your manuscript.

KEN: Right now?

JOE: You don't have to start right now.

JOE: Don't be modest. Thanks to you, Ken, I've finally found my calling in life. I'll be the world's only speed-typing male whore. Six inches and one hundred words per minute. Gives head and takes shorthand too.

KEN: I hope you don't think you're impressing anyone. Sulking is counter-productive.

JOE: If the sight of my idolatry offends you so deeply you could pass me that manuscript. Or you could leave.

KEN: "Idolatry" means "to worship." I don't think that's the word you were looking for.

JOE: You're right. The word I'm looking for is bugger off.

KEN: This is my flat, I'll thank you to remember. My inheritance is the only thing between you and the streets.

JOE: You begged me to come live with you.

KEN: I hardly *begged.* I took pity on you when you had nowhere else to go. I didn't have to invite you to stay here.

JOE: Forgive me, I forgot the hoards of eager young men coming to blows in the streets over who's to share a flat with Ken Halliwell. It's a privilege all right, having one's cock sucked by a bobbing boiled egg!

KEN: The only way I want to see your six inches is six feet under!

(Silence. Then they start giggling, trying hard not to.)

JOE: *(Sobering.)* You never act like you're happy with me.

KEN: *(Astonished.)* Don't I? *(Pause.)* Perhaps it's because I don't have much experience being happy. Sometimes it's hard for me to believe I am. But I am. I'm happy.

(Pause. Then JOE impulsively removes his pants while KEN looks on expectantly. Pants off, JOE bounds onto the bed and strikes a pose designed to entice. KEN, dignified and sedate, sits with him. JOE stretches out with his head in KEN's lap. KEN pushes JOE away.)

Back to your book. Stop pestering me. Kids.

(They sit side by side on the bed for a few moments, reading. JOE leans back and rests his feet in KEN's lap.)

What's this?

JOE: Come across something of interest?

KEN: Nothing you'd know of.

(They continue reading. JOE strokes KEN's face with one foot and plays in his lap with the other.)

This is a new development.

JOE: Care to share it with me?

KEN: It's over your head.

(Pause. JOE tosses his book away.)

JOE: Ken … tell me some more about the Greek gods and goddesses.

KEN: *(Sighs heavily.)* We've been all through that.

JOE: Tell me again.

KEN: I don't know why I put up with you.

(He puts his book aside after carefully marking his place.)

Have I told you the story of Pygmalion and Galatea?

JOE: Tell me again.

KEN: *(Removes JOE's sock.)* Pygmalion was a young, handsome, and brilliant sculptor, famous throughout Cyprus. Only he despised women.

JOE: Sounds like a real catch.

KEN: *(Kissing JOE's toes.)* He had sworn never to marry. His art, he told himself, sufficed to fulfill him. *(Kisses JOE's heel.)* Nevertheless, he devoted his creative genius to sculpting a magnificent statue of a woman, a woman more beautiful than your wildest imaginings. *(Kisses JOE's calf.)* And she grew ever more beautiful the more he worked on her. There had never been woman nor statue in existence lovely as she. Until one day he had to admit to himself *(Kisses JOE's knee.)* that he'd fallen in love with her. His glorious creation. This hopeless love tormented him.

JOE: Poor bloke.

KEN: He kissed the cold, hard, lifeless body all over, caressing the limbs his own had moulded.

(He kisses JOE's thigh. Blackout.)

JOE: What happened next?

Scene Six

(Years later: 1962. Their new flat: the bedroom, as in Scene One, but without the telephone. KEN is sitting on his bed, cutting pictures out of a large art book. Pictures and scraps cover the bed and surrounding floor. JOE is at the desk, typing on the flap of a book's dust-jacket. On his bed is the book with its plastic cover removed, beside it. JOE wears the top of a pair of pyjamas and briefs, KEN the bottoms with no shirt. After a few moments, JOE stops typing and takes out the jacket, reading it over.)

KEN: Did you ever hear back from that publisher.

JOE: *(Goes to his bed with the jacket.)* Yes.

KEN: *(Surprised.)* And?

JOE: *(Replacing the jacket and cover on the book.)* Lots of encouraging notes scribbled on the manuscript. But the verdict was it's too "rarefied" for publication. And you?

KEN: I'm expecting word any day. Though I doubt they'll find it commercially viable.

JOE: *(Examines the book.)* A novel called *Priapus In The Shrubbery* that's not commercially viable? It's unthinkable. *(Holds up the book to KEN.)* There. Can you tell it's been interfered with?

KEN: Give it here.

(JOE throws it to him. KEN examines the book.)

It appears absolutely innocuous. You can't tell anyone's tampered with it until you lay it open.

JOE: *(Grinning.)* Like me.

(KEN tosses it back. JOE places it on a shelf with a pile of others.)

I'm bored, Ken.

KEN: Make up another dirty blurb.

JOE: I've filled the flaps of every volume we nicked. All that's left is to sneak them back in.

KEN: The library's closed now.

JOE: I know. I meant tomorrow. And this time we're waiting around until some unsuspecting undiscriminating member of the reading public picks one up and has the shit shocked out of him. It's no fun being subversive when nobody's paying attention.

KEN: I've been doing some thinking. About where our careers are going.

JOE: What's to think about?

KEN: That's it exactly. Perhaps we were too hasty in deciding to abort our collaborative efforts after *Last Days of Sodom* was rejected.

JOE: It doesn't seem to've injured our anonymity in any way. Besides, I've just started on a new play. When I'm through I want to send it in to the BBC. See what comes of it.

KEN: A play? *(Pause.)* What about?

JOE: Us.

KEN: I'd advise you to abandon that topic in favour of something with a broader commercial appeal—like being strung up by the short hairs.

JOE: Not us as is. *(Pause.)* I took the plot of *The Boy Hairdresser* and converted it into a radio play.

KEN: Isn't that a bit presumptuous? Making use of our manuscripts without first consulting me.

JOE: Rejected manuscripts, Ken. We are as yet prominent members of The Great Unpublished. You should be grateful one at least is being put to some use other than keeping the dust mites company under your bed.

KEN: You're one to expect gratitude, after all I've done for you.

JOE: I thought your intention was for me to gain independence. I wasn't aware that you still wanted *(Searches for an appropriate term.)* ... the Delphic oracle.

KEN: *(Impressed in spite of himself.)* Now *you're* putting words in *my* mouth.

(JOE walks over to KEN and sits in his lap.)

JOE: It's big enough for both of us.

KEN: All the better to accommodate you.

(JOE swings around so he's straddling KEN.)

JOE: Why don't we read to each other. That's always fun. *The Decline and Fall of the Roman Empire*. Why wasn't there one written about "The Rise"?

KEN: *(Setting aside his scissors.)* Too rarefied for publication, no doubt.

(There is a loud knocking on the door.)

Are you expecting someone. *(JOE shakes his head.)* This is odd. We never have unexpected visitors.

JOE: We never have expected visitors. *(He climbs off KEN and moves towards the kitchen door.)* It'll be Mrs. Corden from across the hall. She threatened to come by to tell us all about her holiday seaside.

(More knocking. KEN notices JOE is about to leave the room.)

KEN: Don't leave her on my hands.

(JOE hurriedly grabs a shirt and pants off the floor and goes through the kitchen door, disappearing from sight.)

JOE: *(Off.)* I'm not decent. I have to make myself presentable.

KEN: *(Calling after.)* You'll never get anywhere in life with that attitude.

(Male voices from beyond the door call "Mr. Halliwell? Mr. Orton?" Hearing this KEN looks startled.)

John? *(Pause.)* Shit.

(He goes through the door into the darkness beyond, pulling on a bathrobe. His voice can be heard, off. Also abrasive masculine voices, their words indistinct.)

Oh, dear. Yes, I see. Would you wait here a moment? I'd like a chance to inform my roommate. Mr. Orton, yes.

(KEN comes back into the light looking dazed and frightened. He sees the books, scraps and scissors. In a panic, he gets on his hands and knees and tries to stuff them under the bed. Stops and sits on the bed, near tears.)

(Calling.) John!

JOE: Is it safe to come out?

KEN: I have to speak to you. Now.

(JOE comes in, tucking in his shirt.)

JOE: You look traumatized. What happened? Did she assail you with pictures of herself and Mr. Corden frolicking in their swimming costumes?

KEN: *(In a low hiss.)* There are two police officers at the door. They have a warrant to search the flat.

JOE: Better hide the Vaseline.

KEN: John, I'm serious!

JOE: *(Realizing it's true.)* Calm down, Ken. Maybe it's a mistake. Did they say what this is about?

KEN: Yes.

(Voice calling, "Mr. Halliwell, we're coming in now.")

The books.

JOE: *(Collapses in a chair.)* Oh, shit.

(Lighting shift. In the following KEN acts the part of the prison psychiatrist, interrogating JOE, who squirms beneath a spotlight.)

PSYCHIATRIST: Mr. Orton, I suppose you know why you're here.

JOE: Damaging public property, I'm told.

PSYCHIATRIST: More than simply damaging, Mr. Orton. What fascinates and disturbs me is the time and energy you expended on the ruination of library books.

JOE: We've no circumstances, no means. No money. We wanted those books but couldn't afford them. It made us mad.

PSYCHIATRIST: That doesn't account for the care you put into creating such deranged images. A monkey's face peering from a rose? Dame Sybil Thorndike confronted with a Greco-Roman phallus? Or the so-called "blurbs" you typed in the flaps, deliberately dreadfully misleading the reader as to the books' contents. *(Sounding truly bewildered.)* I simply cannot fathom your reasoning. Why did you do it? Do you even know yourself?

JOE: It's like I said. *(Sheepishly.)* I guess we let our anger get out of hand.

PSYCHIATRIST: You seem a nice, decent young man, Mr. Orton. If you don't mind my saying so, you remind me a bit of my own son. In character alone, you understand. He's been known to get into a few scrapes of his own, I don't mind telling you. But he's basically a good sort.

JOE: That's very flattering, sir

PSYCHIATRIST: Therefore I regret to ask you this. *(Clears his throat.)* What is the nature of your relationship with Mr. Halliwell?

JOE: He's my mate.

> *(Spotlight shifts to KEN, seated. Now JOE takes over as the psychiatrist.)*

KEN: We're lovers.

PSYCHIATRIST: *(Shocked.)* Could you be more specific, Mr. Halliwell?

KEN: You don't want me to get much more specific than that. We live together. Share a flat. We collaborate on a literary basis. We have sex.

PSYCHIATRIST: Do you mean you *want* to … be intimate with Mr. Orton?

KEN: *(Confused.)* Right now?

> *(Pause.)*

PSYCHIATRIST: I won't pretend to understand exactly what you're experiencing, Mr. Halliwell. But I imagine it must entail a great deal of frustration, this … unhealthy idolatry for your young friend. Especially considering he's a family man.

KEN: John? Married? *(Pause.)* Are you delusional, doctor?

PSYCHIATRIST: In fact, he claims you're the one introduced him to his wife.

> *(Pause. KEN is dumbfounded.)*

Well, Mr. Halliwell, I suppose I have all the answers I need from you. All but one. What have you learned from your prison experience?

> *(Pause during which JOE-as-psychiatrist blurs back into JOE-as-himself. He pulls out the handcuffs and attaches himself to KEN.)*

JOE: Chin up, Kenneth. It can't get any worse.

KEN: It's not going to get any better, is it?

    (Tableau. Blackout.)

Act Two

Scene One

(1961: the kitchen. The radio is playing a very early and relent-lessly upbeat Beatles tune. The table is set for two. In the middle of the table is a pathetic assortment of wilted flowers in a cheap vase. KEN is bustling around making breakfast. He's dressed in his pyjamas. JOE enters from the bedroom in his briefs and a T-shirt. He turns off the radio.)

KEN: *(Turning to JOE.)* John! I thought you'd never get up. Sit down, I'll get your tea.

JOE: *(Half-awake.)* What's got you so excited first thing in the morning? Did you have special success wanking off your wake-up hard on?

KEN: *(Sets tea on the table.)* Life. Life has me excited, John.

(He takes JOE by the shoulders and sits him down at the table.)

Drink your tea. I'm fixing breakfast.

JOE: We never have breakfast.

KEN: Well this morning we're having fried eggs, bacon, toast and marmalade.

JOE: How'd you manage that?

KEN: It's all compliments of Miss Boynes from the flat below. I met her as I was picking up the mail. When I mentioned we'd been making do on the dole since *(Allowing himself a moment's irony.) Reading Gaol,* she promptly buried me alive in her benevolence. Although I insisted we're perfectly happy in our picturesque poverty. We don't need much to be content—just each other and a typewriter. Though it would be nice to be able to indulge oneself once in a while. Even with only marmalade.

47

(Pause. KEN looks sad, distant. Then he forces himself to brighten.)
Aren't the flowers lovely, John? She gave them me fresh from her window-box.

JOE: She certainly seems fond of you, Kenneth. Always having you for tea.

KEN: *(As he cooks.)* She's just a lonely old lady.

JOE: An especially unsavoury variety of cunt. She ought to be symbolically immolated.

KEN: She doesn't seem to have any friends. I suppose they've all passed on. Now all she has are her budgerigars, and they keep dying on her too. *(Shrugs.)* She's harmless enough. And the flowers are lovely, John. Just smell them.

JOE: *(Leaning over them warily.)* They're crawling with insects. *(He plucks a spider from a petal, examines it.)* Women should die upon spawning, like spiders, a far nobler species. I can admire spiders.

(He crushes the spider between his fingers.)

KEN: I think they're pretty. Cheery. We need something to liven up this sepulchral atmosphere … *(Puts eggs on their plates.)* Here's your eggs. The toast is coming.

JOE: *(Stares suspiciously at the eggs.)* Was there anything of consequence in the post? A letter from a publisher, perhaps?

KEN: Nothing like that. That's one of the reasons I feel so strangely optimistic this morning. I sent my latest manuscript to yet another publisher only yesterday, so there's no chance I could be receiving a letter of rejection so soon. There *is* a rather mysterious piece of mail addressed to you.

JOE: *(As KEN puts bacon on their plates.)* Mysterious? Then it can't be for me.

KEN: I put it on the desk. Mind the toast.

(KEN goes into the bedroom. The toast immediately pops up, burnt. He returns with the letter.)

JOE: The toast is burnt.

KEN: Shit.

(He hands the letter to JOE, takes the toast and begins scraping off the black part with a knife.)

JOE: *(Reading the envelope.)* Who's "Margaret Ramsey"?

KEN: If you don't know I certainly don't.

(JOE opens up the letter and reads.)

Really, John, now you've decided to take up with *women,* at least make an arrangement with your lovers so they don't send their correspondence to our mutual address. The neighbours will talk. *(Sets toast on plates.)* It's the best I can do.

(JOE leaps up, jolting the table and upsetting the vase, which shatters on the floor. Flowers and water spill everywhere. KEN's food is soaked.)

John! Honestly.

(He gets up and starts to clean up the mess.)

JOE: *(Sits back down in a daze.)* Margaret Ramsey is a play agent. Listen to this: "I was very pleased to receive *Entertaining Mr. Sloane,* which I think is extremely fresh and interesting—"

KEN: *(Interrupting.)* You sent her a copy of *Sloane* and didn't bother telling me?

JOE: *(Gets up and starts pacing.)* I forgot all about it. The BBC producer sent her my radio play when he was through with it. I didn't think anything'd come of it.

KEN: Sit down and eat. Stop leaping about. It's spoiling my appetite.

(JOE takes a swipe at the marmalade, sucking a gob off his finger.)

Does she explicitly state she's wanting to have it produced?

JOE: *(Sits and reads.)* "I'm not absolutely sure it will hold a whole evening but I think it might." *(Looks up.)* That's encouraging, isn't it?

KEN: Eat up. And give me that. *(Takes letter from JOE.)* You're getting it all sticky with marmalade. *(Reads.)* She wants to meet with you.

(JOE leaps up and lunges for the fridge.)

JOE: I know. *(He takes out a bottle of milk.)* You'll come with me, won't you?

(Swigs.)

KEN: Don't drink milk from the bottle. *(He pours a glass of milk for JOE.)* Are you certain Miss Ramsey would appreciate my presence?

JOE: If she doesn't she can fuck her extremely fresh and interesting self.

(KEN is reasonably satisfied by this answer, but continues to fuss.)

KEN: Who's going to clean up this mess.

JOE: I made the mess, I'll clean it up.

(JOE takes a dish rag and starts wiping up the table with a dramatic flourish.)

Look, I'm Kenneth Halliwell.

KEN: *(Scowling.)* That's not the way you do it. You're spilling crumbs all over my *(With self-conscious irony.) nice clean floor.*

(Takes the rag from JOE.)

Your problem, John, is that you do everything for dramatic effect, at the cost of practical results. Now, watch: *(Demonstrating.)* Take the rag and wipe the crumbs into the palm of your hand, cupped and placed like so.

(JOE comes up behind KEN and seizes KEN's crotch.)

JOE: Cupped and placed—like so?

KEN: You never cease to amaze yourself.

JOE: *(Grabs the letter from KEN.)* I'm so overcome I think I'll have a piss to celebrate. *(He heads for the lavatory with the letter.)* I knew it had to happen eventually. I *knew.* Didn't you?

(Pause. KEN doesn't respond.)

Ken? Didn't you always know?

(JOE disappears from sight. KEN takes out the broom and dust-pan, starts sweeping up the shattered vase.)

KEN: *(Not at all certain.)* Of course I knew.

(Lights fade.)

Scene Two

(1966. JOE sits on his bed, talking. He looks, and sounds, completely exhausted. KEN moves around in the background, unpacking JOE's suitcase. JOE is in his jeans and T-shirt; KEN wears his pyjamas.)

JOE: … the lead actress becoming hysterical and having to be led off stage, taken home and sedated. Irate old bitches tearing their programs to bits in the aisles. Conversations overheard in the lobby during intermission: "It's about Jesus, d'you see, being a queer." Christ! It was a farce all right but no one was laughing. Me least of all. The director took me out to dinner one night towards the end. Ostensibly to discuss his new technique of having the actors speak in time with a metronome. To "emphasize style." I suppose in the hope that the content might be politely overlooked. "You can't communicate,

Joe," he said to me. "It's your one great flaw as an artist and as a human being," he said. I told him to manœuver his metronome up his middle-class ass and asked if I'd communicated my meaning to his satisfaction. Well no I didn't but I wish I had. Perhaps he's right. I've rewritten the play beyond recognition or redemption. When I try to sleep I dream I'm still rewriting in some nondescript hotel room, each one as hostile to compulsory inspiration as the one previous, at that fucking portable typewriter, the only consistent element. It kept me from bouncing off the nondescript walls. Along with your letters. Why didn't you ring me, Ken? I know it must have been lonely here. But you know all I could think of was getting home. *(Looks up at KEN whose expression is inscrutable.)* To your welcoming arms and your comforting words, I think it was. *(Pause. No response.)* Or your welcoming words and your comforting arms. *(Pause.)* All right, if you're not going to comfort me you could at least pity me. Out loud, if you please.

(JOE lies back on the bed. KEN stands over him and looks down.)

KEN: Moan moan moan. That's all it ever is from you. This room isn't big enough for two Lady Macbeths.

JOE: I could always clasp an asp to my bosom.

KEN: Asps are so passé. Besides, the poor creature would probably die of boredom. It would be far more practical if you'd settle for gouging out your eyes with a butter knife. Only you'll have to hold off on the gouging-out bit till I get around to doing the dishes. Can't have you committing suicide with soiled silverware.

JOE: I've already told Peggy I shan't continue like this. I can't work under these circumstances.

KEN: Remember when we had no circumstances? You didn't go around swooning and moaning then.

JOE: I'm beginning to take myself too seriously, in your opinion.

KEN: In my opinion, yes. But perhaps I've caught you just in time. In the act, as it were. What we both need is a change of scenery. To be specific: a holiday.

JOE: *(Dazed.)* A holiday ...

KEN: Away from the miserable, typical, fog-and-pissing-rain weather as well as the misty memories, I can recover from the blow Peggy Ramsey dealt me.

JOE: You were attacked by my agent?

KEN: The wounds are figurative only. *(Pause.)* She rejected my play.

JOE: Ken, I'm sorry. I know how hard you worked. *(Pause.)* Did she have anything positive to say?

KEN: She did mention it was unique in one respect.

JOE: There you go.

KEN: She said it was so unbearably boring she couldn't force herself to read the whole thing. The rejection was based upon the first scene. She suggested I enter into a profession better suited to my literary abilities—like dentistry.

JOE: She didn't.

KEN: Shall I produce her commentary?

JOE: *(Almost amused in spite of himself.)* I'll have to have a talk with her.

KEN: I don't need you to defend my honour. I'd rather confront the truth of what people think of me.

JOE: Peggy thinks a great deal of you. You mustn't let her wording put you off. When she first read *Sloane* she told me she found it derivative.

KEN: Perhaps she had that in mind when she called my play "drivel."

JOE: You can't let this—

KEN: *(Shrieking.)* Shut up! Just shut up, would you? And don't expect me to be sympathetic and comforting when you start going on about "renouncing the theatre." *You* have a choice.

JOE: You have real talent—

KEN: *(Near tears.)* And don't say that! I don't want to hear that anymore, do you understand me? You *knew,* didn't you. *(Pause. JOE avoids looking at him.)* You knew the play was shit. You just wanted to watch me humiliate myself.

JOE: You know that isn't true. You know I want you to succeed.

KEN: *(Gaining momentum.)* Why? Because you think you owe me? Because you want to unburden yourself of your misguided guilt?

JOE: Try because I *love* you.

KEN: *(Out of control.)* There *is* a God!

   (Pause.)

JOE: I don't know what more you want.

KEN: A church wedding.

JOE: I just told you I loved you. Out loud. To your face. With my clothes on. What is it you want? Me to prove it to you? Because I will. Because I do owe you, Ken, and I want to help you.

KEN: What can you do? Unless it's true the rumour you parted the Red Sea with your prick.

JOE: There's still your collages. Whenever we've anyone in it's the first thing they remark upon. That reporter who was here the other day, he was so busy admiring them and going on about how "professional" they look I had to remind him of his reason for coming.

KEN: *(Sulking.)* How would I know that? You exile me from the flat whenever you're being interviewed.

JOE: That's why I'm telling you. I have influence now; connections, you know. *(Remembering.)* That's if I've a reputation left after this apocalyptic production. I still think *Loot* can be a success. I think it's the best thing I've written. You thought so too, remember? If it's ever given a proper production—*(He notices KEN's expression and stops. Defensively.)* Well after all, the play's the thing. D'you like that? I just made it up. *(Pause.)* Ken. Let me arrange a showing for you.

KEN: I've failed at everything else I've undertaken. Why should this be any different?

JOE: *(Bluntly.)* I don't know.

KEN: Thank you for admitting that.

JOE: Would you rather I patronize you?

KEN: I'm not asking to be patronized. I'd be content with an outdated display of conjugal support.

JOE: *(With disdain.)* "Conjugal support"—it sounds like a type of brassiere.

KEN: Of course I know what intense distaste such terms inspire in you. I know how necessary it is for you to believe everything in your life is disposable. Temporary. Transitory. It's just a stage.

JOE: The whole world's a stage. *(Pause.)* Where would we go? If we had our holiday.

KEN: *(Suddenly excited.)* I've already thought of that. I made some inquiries while you were in Cambridge. Tangier's the answer. Everyone who's been raves like mad about it. Think of it—scantily clad Moroccan boys swarming the beaches. And all available!

JOE: I think we've found your calling, Ken. Ever consider becoming a travel agent?

KEN: I'm told in confidence the boys'll do anything for a scant few dirhans. They *all* take it, or so I hear.

JOE: But you don't ask them to do anything. *(Over KEN's protests.)* Mutual masturbation and other dormitory schoolboy antics.

KEN: I didn't mention me specifically. I was making the point that they'll do anything for *your* benefit. And for your knowledge I've been fucked without a qualm by various other parties. It's *you* who has the sexual block.

JOE: Only with you.

KEN: And for a second it slipped my mind I'm living with the connoisseur of London's low-life. A connoisseur of sewage.

JOE: Save the rest of it for a time when I can appreciate it. Or throw it back. *(Starts to remove his jeans.)* I'm so tired right now I don't even know what I'm saying. I don't want to talk about sex.

KEN: Now I believe you're tired.

(KEN starts helping JOE off with his jeans.)

JOE: *(Moans.)* Ken, I just *said—*

KEN: Oh give your whining a rest. I'm not partial to necrophilia.

(He folds the jeans and socks neatly and drapes them over the back of a chair. Takes the blanket from his own bed and gently tucks it around JOE, who's lying on top of the covers. He sits on a chair by the bed, watching JOE.)

JOE: *(Without opening his eyes.)* Ken?

KEN: Go to sleep.

JOE: We have to get you a wig.

KEN: *(Feels his bald head.)* A wig?

JOE: So that when we get to Morocco, the boys won't mistakenly think they're wanking off the King and I instead of an old queen.

(KEN gets up and turns out the lights. Lighting change. He sits back down.)

KEN: John? *(No answer. He forces himself to use the new name.)* Joe. Doesn't it ever frighten you? The futility of it. Anonymous sex with indifferent strangers. *(Quickly.)* I just want to know. *(Pause.)* I need to know. *(Pause.)* You owe me that.

JOE: *(Sits up a little and stares at KEN.)* What is it you think you'll get out of me, Confessor 'Iggins? Come back and see me on my deathbed. Maybe then you'll get what you want. But only maybe.

KEN: Everyone's afraid. You can't tell me you're not.

JOE: What if I told you there's no room in me to be frightened—nothing left of me to be scared. I'm too fucking angry.

KEN: I know you are. I am too.

JOE: Not like I am.

KEN: I know. Why are you so angry.

JOE: *(Sitting up fully.)* Why *aren't* you? What are *you* so frightened of, Ken? What is it about what I do that scares you so much you can't even be as angry as you should be? It's not the danger, the risks involved. Not that alone. And it's not the fear that I'll form an emotional attachment in the space of a few hours spent sweating and moaning, because we both know that won't happen.

KEN: That's it. It's your attitude. You're so cold. Hard. *You* frighten me. When did it happen? When did you change? *(Pause.)* Did I do this?

JOE: *(Mocking.)* Don't torment yourself.

KEN: I'm scared. It's true. But so are you—I know you are. *(Pause. A realization.)* You're afraid of *real intimacy.*

JOE: *(With intensity, but without emotion.)* And you're a fucking elitist snob. Men forced to seek each other out to suck each other off in shadows, dark corners, and derelict houses, always wary, ever alert, always predatory. However much you whine and bitch you're always willing to listen to my grim fairy tales so long as there's a punch line. Then you can afford to be amused, reassured of the fact that you're "above" that sort of behaviour. That *is* what you think, isn't it?

KEN: *(With dignity.)* Yes. It is.

JOE: And I'm the heartless bastard. Do you understand what it is to be forced into a position that offers no options, no alternatives, no *choice?*

KEN: *(Turns to JOE and takes his hand.)* But John, you *do* have another choice.

JOE: *(Yanks his hand away.)* So I do.

   (He turns over to face the wall. KEN continues to sit staring.)

Scene Three

(Lighting change. Same set as above; same positions.)

KEN: My mother died when I was eleven.

JOE: *(Rising from the bed.)* Oh Christ, here it comes. Run for cover.

KEN: Shut up. I'm trying to illicit some sympathy here.

(JOE pulls out the handcuffs, and clasps himself to KEN. They sit side by side, JOE on the bed, KEN on a chair, facing the audience.)

JOE: It's "Pity Ken" time. If you let him go on he'll never stop.

KEN: *(Ignoring him.)* My mother died of a wasp sting. It bit her in the mouth. She was dead in a matter of minutes. I know because I was there. I watched her suffocate. There was nothing I could do. I was eleven. *(To JOE.)* There, I think I handled that with a reasonable amount of dignity. Nothing maudlin in my delivery.

JOE: I wasn't listening. Get to your father, did you?

KEN: No, I was saving that.

JOE: Allow me. His father stuck his head in an oven twelve years later.

KEN: I found him when I came down for breakfast.

JOE: He didn't bother with a note.

KEN: We never communicated much.

JOE: So he turned off the gas—

KEN: Safety first.

JOE: Put on the kettle—

KEN: For my morning tea.

JOE: Shaved—

KEN: And called the police. *(Pause. To JOE.)* Do they look sympathetic to you?

JOE: It might've been more diplomatic to omit the parts about the shaving and tea-drinking.

KEN: Oh well. It was an honest effort.

JOE: I learnt diplomacy from my mum.

KEN: She was the Perfect Wife and Mother.

JOE: At least when she had an audience. We kids were essential to her performance.

KEN: The props she put on display.

JOE: When the curtain came down we ceased to exist.

KEN: In theory.

JOE: In reality we cramped her style, always underfoot, always doing something embarrassing like forgetting our lines.

KEN: Or straying from the script.

JOE: If the curtain ever came down around her ears she wouldn't've noticed.

KEN: She would've pretended it was part of the act.

JOE: I learnt to improvise from my mum, too. If life hands you a pile of shit you make lemonade.

KEN: And smile whilst you're drinking it, too.

JOE: *(Becoming agitated.)* My father fit right in as he only existed in theory to begin with.

KEN: He behaved like an inanimate object and that's how she treated him.

JOE: *(Gaining momentum.)* We kids had no choice, you see, but he *allowed* her to carry on the way she did. I wish once he would've belted her.

KEN: She was wanting it.

JOE: *(Out of control.)* Just once he should've hit her hard enough she'd realize he was alive! He should've—

KEN: Bashed her brains out in her bed?

  (Blackout.)

Scene Four

(1966. KEN is in his chair, JOE asleep in bed. The handcuffs are gone. KEN is reading JOE's journal. The phone rings. JOE bolts upright in bed. He sees KEN; sees the diary. They stare at each other a moment. Then JOE gets out of bed and answers the phone.)

JOE: Hello. It's Joe. Yes. I understand. *(Hangs up. Pause.)* That was George.

KEN: *(Setting the journal on the desk.)* Your sister's husband. Why'd he pick this hour to suddenly start extending familial courtesies?

JOE: My mum's dead.

KEN: Joe.

JOE: Bugger didn't say when the funeral's to be. I'll have to telegram for details.

KEN: I remember what it was like when my mother died.

JOE: Oh no. We're not getting into that. This is *my* problem, these are *my* feelings. Go tell yours to your analyst. I'm going back to sleep.

KEN: Do you want to talk?

JOE: *(Suddenly vulnerable, on the verge of tears.)* I just wish … I wish we'd had an … opportunity to overcome our … past differences and … come to understand each other's circumstances as … rational, adult human beings.

KEN: *(Moves to comfort him.)* Joe, don't—

    (JOE shoves KEN away. His voice is cold. The tears were fake.)

JOE: Only I don't write that way, Kenneth. I don't feel that way. All this means to my life is I'm going to have to spend a couple of days bidding farewell to the corpse of a woman I never knew and avoiding sobbing relatives who did and didn't give a shit while she was alive. Not everybody can play the martyr as definitively as you.

KEN: I'm not—

JOE: And you're not going to. I won't let you. You're jealous of everything in my life, including the death of my blessed mum, may she roast in peace. I'm not letting you have this. It's mine; I'll deal with it my way.

KEN: You're in pain—

JOE: I'm indifferent. Your mother sprang this mortal coil thirty years ago. It's time you got over it. I'm already over mine.

    (JOE turns to face the wall again. Blackout.)

Scene Five

    (The bedroom. KEN is once again unpacking for JOE, who's playing with a pair of dentures.)

KEN: Did you reach out and extract them from the jaws of death whilst everyone else kept occupied reflecting on life's tragic transience? Or did she bequeath them to you in her will, as her legacy?

JOE: Found them in a drawer, to tell the prosaic truth.

KEN: A little token to remember her by. It's your sentimental side making itself apparent.

JOE: I'm going to show them to the cast. Give them a taste of the real thing. They need to be shocked out of their smug complacency.

KEN: Why? It doesn't seem to've done us much good. *(Pause.)* How was the funeral?

JOE: It was a moan. The floral arrangements and eulogy alike displayed a depressing lack of creativity. If I hadn't happened upon these teeth the whole weekend would've been a loss. I did have some good sex though.

KEN: With whom? A precocious choirboy, was it, or a carnally inclined vicar?

JOE: Vicarious fucking is more your area, isn't it? I got mine in on the way to and from. *(Pause.)* Did you see that clipping that came in the post this morning? It said I'd written the best play of 1966, called "Loo." *(Pause.)* Don't look so amused, Kenneth. Wouldn't want anyone to suspect such mundane, inept humdrummery actually tickled you.

KEN: I'm supposed to find it amusing that the papers can't even spell the names of your plays correctly? The only fucking thing I visibly contribute to that fucking play and they have to go fucking it up.

JOE: It's shocking, all right! You ought to write a letter of complaint. It's a tradition amongst bored housewives with nothing better to do.

KEN: I have plenty of things better to do. For instance, I could sit here graciously tolerating your prattle all day.

(The phone rings.)

JOE: Or you could answer the phone.

KEN: You know very well there hasn't been a single phone call for me since you installed that instrument of torture.

JOE: Come now, Ken. You know the only reason I had it installed was the same reason that purblind reporter made his sadistic spelling error: to torment you. In fact, that's the only reason anything happens around here. It's the reason the world keeps turning. You mustn't disappoint your many fans.

(Pause. JOE is nonchalant, KEN agitated. Finally KEN jumps up and answers the phone.)

KEN: *(With exaggerated gaiety.)* Joe Orton's residence! *(Pause.)* Hello, Peggy. Yes, it's me. Joe hasn't bothered to acquire an anatomically accurate housemaid yet. Joe has very low personal standards of living.

JOE: *(To the teeth.)* Look what I live with.

KEN: *(Into phone.)* Yes, he's right here. Me? Why even ask? You know I'm always happy, fulfilled and thrilled with the state of my life. Joe's enthusiastic nature rubs off on me. And so does he occasionally. *(Pause.)* Hold on, I'll ask. *(To JOE.)* Peggy wants to know if we're still dedicated to going through with our "little Moroccan adventure."

JOE: Tell Peggy we're leaving as soon as we can find somewhere reasonable to stay far from the omnipresent glare of Moroccan law enforcement.

KEN: *(Into phone.)* Joe says yes. *(Pause. To JOE.)* Peggy says I'll have to look out for you. "Don't want anything unforeseen befalling my number-one commodity," she says. "One hears of such dreadful goings-on in these free-living foreign countries," Peggy says.

JOE: Fuck "Peggy says."

KEN: *(Into phone.)* Joe thanks you for your concern. All right. One second. *(To JOE.)* Peggy says she has some exciting news for you.

(JOE yawns, stretches, rises reluctantly and saunters languidly across the room to take the phone.)

JOE: She wasn't so concerned the last time we pissed off to Tangier. Now *Loot*'s been remounted a success suddenly she's afraid to let me go to the lavatory by myself. *(Takes phone.)* Hi, Peggy, how are you? Ken is fine. He's just experiencing an allergic reaction to all those laurel leaves gracing his brow. *(Pause.)* Yes. Yes, I know. Yes, Peggy. Peggy—yes. It's not like we're venturing into volatile enemy territory. We returned from our last visit unscathed, aside from the obligatory sunburns and venereal diseases, both of which I bore with pride. *No,* I will *not* be working on the play. I intend this holiday to be dedicated to sun, boys, and hashish. The only reason I'm taking the typewriter along is so I can put the trip down as a tax write-off, "gathering information for a play," that sort of thing. Yes. That's a good idea. *(To KEN, who has his back to JOE.)* Peggy says I should use you as a tax write-off, too. Put you down as my "personal assistant."

(JOE holds out the receiver expectantly.)

KEN: *(Mimicking.)* Fuck "Peggy says."

(He turns in time to see what JOE has done.)

JOE: *(Into phone.)* Right. *(To KEN, chiding.)* She heard that.

KEN: Tell Peggy I'm just being a queen. My crown's a size too small.

JOE: It's the size of your scepter I'd be worried about. *(Into phone.)* Ken's apologies. What's the big news? *(Pause as JOE listens.)* Yes. Well that is exciting then. Right. Happy? I'm fucking on air! *(He suddenly notices that KEN has become curious. Forcing himself to be casual.)* Yes, we've heard. Yes well I suppose it would, Peggy, only I prefer to fuck fourteen-year-olds. *(Pause.)* Ring me as soon as you know then. *(Hangs up phone. To KEN, casually.)* Peggy congratulates us on the new over-twenty-one law. *(Pause.)* Dinner ready?

> *(KEN glares at him, then gets up and heads for the kitchen. Blurts it out.)*

> *Loot* has won the Evening Standard Drama Award for best play of the year.

KEN: *(Truly impressed.)* Joe, that's … My God.

JOE: *(Allowing himself to become excited.)* You do realize what this will mean at the box office? It's precisely the boost we needed. The stalls'll be packed tighter than the Pope's arsehole once word of the award gets out. I'm to appear on the television for the attending ceremony. You'll have to help me with the acceptance speech.

KEN: *(Considering.)* The occasion requires something that'll sound spontaneously witty and gracious but not *too* humble.

JOE: I'm not very good at that.

KEN: Which, sounding gracious or being humble?

JOE: Both. That's what I need you for. What shall I wear? We've nothing suitable for the telly. You'll have to help me pick something out. Something loud. Ken—*we've done it.*

> *(Pause.)*

KEN: *(In a hollow voice.)* Will it say that on the trophy.

JOE: What do you mean?

KEN: I'm asking if the trophy will bear the names "Joe Orton and Kenneth Halliwell."

JOE: Of course not.

KEN: Then whence this "we"?

JOE: Both of us know I couldn't've written it without you.

KEN: Two people in the entire world who know that. And I'm not absolutely convinced I'm not a figment of your imagination.

JOE: I've always acknowledged how much you help me.

KEN: To *me* you've acknowledged it. You're preaching to your sole convert. What would please me would be if you got up on that platform in front of God, the television cameras, your precious peers and everyone, *"We'd* like to thank all the little people out there without whom none of this would be possible …"Instead you include me in that category.

JOE: You'll always be a big pain in the arse to me, Kenneth. *(Pause.)* Come with me to the ceremony. I'm required to bring a guest. Peggy said.

KEN: *(Stiffly.)* Ask Peggy. I'm sure she'll be enchanted. As for me, nothing on earth could entice me to attend such a funereal affair.

JOE: I seem to sense we're having some domestic problems.

KEN: Oedipus had domestic problems. We're dead fucked. *(He starts rummaging through the desk drawers.)* Have you seen my pills? I need my pills.

(JOE goes into the kitchen. KEN finds the jar of pills: different shapes and colours mixed together. He also takes out his compact. He swallows a few pills. Opens up the compact and peers into it. He addresses his reflection while dabbing some rouge on his face.)

How do you do? I'm Kenneth Halliwell. No, you won't have heard of me. I'm Joe Orton's personal assistant. But you can just call me his bitter half. Joe's accepting the award for play of the year. Yes, he's the one wrote *Loot*. Only the title is mine. Did you know? No, you wouldn't have. All the titles are mine, all the trophies are his. Also, he's wearing my suit. I don't mind. He wears it well.

(He stares hard at himself for a moment. Then he snaps the compact shut and lets it drop on the floor. He crushes it beneath his foot, as if extinguishing a cigarette.)

Smashing.

(He picks up the jar of pills. Looks around to make sure JOE isn't in sight, and starts over.)

Hello, how do you do? Kenneth Halliwell. The pleasure's all mine. You won't have heard of me. I'm accepting the award on Joe Orton's behalf. Best play of the year, yes. I'm so glad you like it. Joe would be too, only he's dead. Unfortunate accident. His typewriter tripped—and fell on his head! Splat. Dreadful machines. Ought to bear a warning label.

JOE: *(Off.)* Ken? Are you saying something?

(KEN starts, dropping the jar. The pills spill all over the floor. He gets down on his hands and knees, grabs them in handfuls and dumps them on the bed.)

(Entering.) They're not in the kitchen. *(He sees KEN.)* What're you doing? I wouldn't go committing suicide were I you. You'll have nothing left to hold over my head.

KEN: I'll do it one of these days and then where will you be?

JOE: Fuck you. You're not ruining this for me. *(He puts on his jacket.)* I'm going out. I can't listen to this again.

KEN: You'd leave me when I'm like this?

JOE: I'm doing us both a fucking lot of good by staying, is that it?

KEN: Go, then! But don't be surprised if I'm gone when you get back.

JOE: I'll make it a point not to be.

KEN: *(Wailing.)* Look what you're doing to me!

JOE: I don't want to look. I can't look. I'm going out.

KEN: Who wants you here?

JOE: That's what I'd like to know.

KEN: Don't come back!

JOE: *(Mimicking.)* One of these days I won't and then where will you be?

KEN: You know the answer to that!

(JOE start to go.)

Joe!

(He pauses in the doorway.)

You are coming back, aren't you?

JOE: After fifteen years you still don't know the answer?

(KEN has no response. JOE puts on his cap and leaves. Blackout.)

Scene Six

(KEN is at the typewriter. He's wearing his wig. JOE comes in wearing his jacket and carrying a record album.)

JOE: What're you doing at the typewriter?

KEN: I didn't realize I needed a specific reason to use my own typewriter.

JOE: I was making conversation. I didn't realize I needed special permission to inquire after your activities.

KEN: As it happens, I'm composing a letter to Peggy—about my artwork. Since she seemed so intrigued by the little she's seen. How *is* Peggy?

JOE: Same old. I told her I've started a diary. She was most pleased, going on as she does. *(He puts the record on the turntable.)* "The publishers will simply eat it up, dear. *Eat it up!" (Pause. The music begins: "Sgt. Pepper.")* She wants to know if you're keeping a journal as well. As she suggested.

KEN: *(Quoting Miss Prism.)* "Memory is the diary we all carry around with us." I have a hard enough time remembering everything I want to forget without writing it down. *(Irritably.)* What's that?

JOE: The Beatles' new one. *(He hands KEN the sleeve.)* I thought you might find the cover of interest. It's a collage.

KEN: *(Studies it.)* Look! There's Oscar Wilde.

JOE: Where?

KEN: *(Points.)* Behind John.

JOE: Dirty old bastard. *(Pause.)* Who d'you imagine's the more famous?

KEN: Now or in the long run? Oscar met with a premature end. That's always a boon to fame. Or infamy. *(Innocently.)* Where are you?

JOE: *(As he heads for the kitchen.)* Oh ye of little phallus. I'll get there yet.

    (JOE disappears into the kitchen.)

KEN: *(Calling to JOE.)* Perhaps Peggy can be of some assistance. God knows that so-called "show" you arranged for me wasn't. Stuck in a smelly basement up the arse-end of the King's Road.

JOE: *(From the kitchen.)* I tried, Ken. I'm still trying. The other day I received an invitation to view some modern art at some gallery or other.

KEN: Why would they want a playwright to look at their artwork?

JOE: It's my name they're after. Well I hope it's not my money. They can't expect I'll purchase any of their abstract rubbish. I'm only going because it might help you.

KEN: Poor Joe. The weight of the world in your pants.

    (Sounds of the fridge door being slammed and JOE angrily banging around.)

Don't take it out on the household appliances. It's always the innocents that suffer.

JOE: *(Sticking his head through the doorway.)* There's nothing to eat.

KEN: So go to the shops. Unless your status as an established playwright has impaired your ability to shop for food.

JOE: *(Sauntering back into the room.)* Paul McCartney says John has forgotten how to use the phone he's had others doing it for him so long.

KEN: Did he tell you that in person?

JOE: No. I read it somewhere.

KEN: Myself I read in some magazine that one can tell a great deal about a person by having them name their favourite Beatle. I told this to my psychiatrist and he said, "Very well, Kenneth. Who is your favourite Beatle?"

JOE: And you said?

KEN: And I said, "I have no opinion about them, actually. But Joe says Paul McCartney's a delightful chap."

JOE: You should've told him I said he was a delightful fuck.

KEN: Joe! *(Curious.)* He's not that way, is he?

JOE: *(In mock-horror.)* Heavens no! What're you thinking of? The Beatles—fairies? You're talking about the disfigured heads of a cultural revolution.

KEN: You're still sore because they rejected your film script.

JOE: My dignity was injured, it's true. But who needs dignity who has a senile producer offering to buy a rejected screenplay for a ridiculous sum.

KEN: Doris has sold her flat. The Cordens will be next. Everyone's moving on but us.

JOE: Why not us?

KEN: I was just thinking the same thing. In fact, I've already begun perusing properties in the paper.

JOE: I could keep this flat to work in, and purchase a house to live in properly.

KEN: *(Suddenly and viciously.)* I haven't shit in two days! What do you think it means?

> *(JOE involuntarily clutches at his temples. He goes to the turntable and takes the needle off the record.)*

JOE: What did you expect? You haven't eaten anything in a week. You just keep sucking milk through a straw. It's creepy.

KEN: My digestion isn't functioning properly. I can't eat solid food.

JOE: I'm sick of discussing your digestion.

KEN: *(Stuffily.)* I'm sorry if the subject of my health isn't one best-suited to hold your interest, but it is a source of great concern to me.

JOE: I'll start being concerned when there's something wrong with you you're not doing to yourself.

KEN: I suppose you're wanting dinner.

JOE: I told you there's nothing to eat. Anyway I'm going out tonight, remember? To the Lord Mayor of London's banquet.

KEN: Is that tonight? *(Pause.)* Look in the cupboard for a can of sardines. There might be one left. It's not likely you'll find anything edible at your rubbishy dinner.

JOE: Oh, I don't know. It's rumoured they serve an excellent turtle soup.

KEN: You must bring me some home in a doggy bag.

JOE: *(Pauses in the doorway.)* Want one?

KEN: *(Shudders.)* No. *(Pause.)* You're not wearing that.

JOE: *(Coming back into the room.)* I'll wear my good shirt. And my old suit. Unless you'd—

KEN: No.

JOE: Why not? You never wear them. They just rot in the closet.

KEN: That's not the point. They're still mine. I bought them with my own money.

> *(Pause.)*

JOE: I have to get a new suit. Several new suits.

KEN: And new shirts. *(Pause.)* And socks. All your socks have holes in them. If you can afford a new house you can afford a new pair of socks to go to the Lord Mayor's banquet.

JOE: Too late now.

> *(He wiggles his toes, which stick out of the holes in his socks.)*

I'm fond of my socks.

KEN: They're disgusting. Old, torn and worn.

JOE: Dirty socks are kinky, like dirty underwear. Dirty socks, dirty sex. *(Pause.)* I remember a time when my holes weren't so distasteful to you.

KEN: I remember indulging you because of your youth. You no longer have that as an excuse.

> *(JOE looks through the closet. Takes out a shirt and holds it up.)*

JOE: There's a hole in my shirt. *(Sticks his hand through.)* My best shirt. And my only clean good shirt. How did this happen?

KEN: I can't imagine. Are you certain you didn't tear it during one of your flirtations with the forbidden and forgot about it in the heat of the moment? Try to think back. Perhaps it would refresh your memory if I were to flush the toilet a few times.

JOE: I wouldn't wear my good shirt out cottaging. For one thing it'd make me look poncy.

KEN: *(Suddenly accommodating.)* I'll have it mended, Joe. In the meantime borrow one of mine.

JOE: Why would you want to have it mended?

KEN: Because it's torn.

JOE: I mean, *I* could have it mended.

KEN: Suit yourself.

JOE: Is there any special reason you'd want to have my shirt mended?

KEN: I don't need a special reason to have a torn shirt mended!

> *(Pause.)*

I know what this is about.

JOE: Just lend me one of your shirts and shut up.

KEN: Don't think for a moment you're fooling me.

JOE: Lend me a shirt.

KEN: You think I tore your shirt.

JOE: *(Warning.)* Ken.

KEN: You honestly think I've nothing better to do than sit in this room tearing holes in your clothing for entertainment.

JOE: I don't want to fight with you over a fucking shirt.

KEN: We're not fighting—yet. But if we were—just supposing—we'd be fighting over the fact that *you think I tore your shirt!*

JOE: I didn't say that.

KEN: You didn't have to.

JOE: *(Lying.)* I didn't think that.

KEN: Now you're lying.

JOE: Now we're fighting.

KEN: *(Shouting.)* No we are *not!*

> *(Pause.)*

JOE: I can't say I wasn't expecting this. The relative peace we've known since our return had an ominous tinge to it. I knew it couldn't last. *(Pause.)* You were happy in Tangier. I like seeing you happy.

KEN: That was then and there. This is here and now. Life only makes sense in terms of the here and now. And sometimes not even then.

JOE: It's still the same us.

KEN: It's different.

JOE: What can I do—

KEN: There's nothing you can do! Just accept what is.

JOE: I won't live like this.

KEN: Not much longer.

JOE: I can't.

KEN: You don't have to.

JOE: I don't want to feel the way you do.

KEN: Do you think I do?

JOE: But I want to understand the way you feel.

KEN: You think I don't?

JOE: *Do you?*

KEN: The honeymoon's over. The holiday's over. Everything's back to normal. We just have to … adjust.

JOE: Fuck our normal! I want out.

KEN: What about me?

JOE: You'll adjust.

KEN: *(Out of control.)* You're *committed* … you … stupid … *cunt!* *We're* committed.

> *(Pause.)*

JOE: *(Frigidly.)* One of us should be. And if bets were being placed—

KEN: They'd be on me like flies on feces?

JOE: Just lend me a shirt.

KEN: First admit it.

JOE: Admit what?

KEN: What you were thinking.

JOE: Give me a shirt.

KEN: First admit it.

JOE: Admit what? *What am I guilty of?*

KEN: Admit that you think I tore your shirt.

JOE: First *give me a shirt.*

> *(Pause. They glare at each other. KEN, in a rage, grabs several shirts from the closet and throws them at JOE.)*

KEN: *(Screaming.) I hate you!*

JOE: *(Going through the shirts.)* Thank you. *(He picks one out and puts it on.)* The thought had crossed my mind.

KEN: What thought.

JOE: That you tore my shirt. It's human nature. I have to go now. Peggy's picking me up.

> *(He moves to go. KEN clutches at his sleeve.)*

KEN: Give me my shirt back.

JOE: *(Jerking away.)* What's the matter with you?

KEN: With me?

JOE: There's nothing wrong with me but you.

KEN: That's not true.

JOE: It is.

KEN: Well I did.

JOE: Did what?

KEN: Tear your shirt.

JOE: I know. Why?

KEN: You know why.

JOE: Second-best?

KEN: While we're being honest.

JOE: Go on!

KEN: Just tell me.

JOE: Tell you what.

KEN: Do you love me or not.

JOE: It's not that simple.

KEN: Grow up, Joe! It *is* that simple.

> *(Long pause.)*

> Oh. Oh, my God.

JOE: It's not what you think.

KEN: *(Searching frantically.)* My pills.

JOE: I'm trying to … I'm trying—

KEN: Shut up. I don't want to hear it. Do you understand?

JOE: I won't leave you.

KEN: It's up to you, John.

JOE: Joe.

KEN: Who?

JOE: Me.

KEN: What?

JOE: It's my name. Joe. You said "John."

KEN: *(Dazed.)* Did I?

JOE: It's been three years now. It's not as though I changed something of great import, like my sex.

KEN: If you'd had a sex change I'd have no trouble keeping it straight. As it is, I forget. *(With sarcastic emphasis.)* Joe.

JOE: *(Pleasantly.)* Yes, Kenneth?

KEN: You wanted to know what all this is about. I'm telling you. It's all about names.

JOE: How is it about names?

KEN: I'm coming to that. I'll tell you, but first you have to do something for me.

JOE: Name it.

KEN: Take off that shirt.

JOE: Ken.

KEN: I'm not letting you borrow it. I've changed my mind. I'm being fickle. Pretend my spontaneity amuses you. I'm the spice in your life. Or the fly in your K-Y. Take it off.

JOE: I don't have time for this shit.

KEN: Take off that fucking shirt or I'll tear it from you.

> *(JOE removes the shirt in a fury, ripping it in the process. Buttons fly; KEN cringes. JOE puts on the torn shirt and a suit jacket over that.)*

> *(As JOE is changing.)* Now I'll tell you about names. Witness my signature.

> *(He shows JOE the paper he was typing on.)*

JOE: *(Reads.)* "Kenneth Halliwell, Secretary to Joe Orton." So?

KEN: I've never signed myself as your secretary before. There's something wrong with that signature and we both of us know what it is. That's not your name, *John.* And I'm not your secretary.

JOE: Yes you are. And yes, I *am.* Joe Orton. That's who I am. Live with it.

KEN: I won't … I won't accept that …

JOE: It's up to you. In the meantime I'm going out to dinner. Smile and pretend you're happy for me and maybe I'll come back.

> *(KEN glares at him.)*

Come on, Ken. Smile and pretend.

KEN: *(Turning his back to JOE, with dignity.)* I dislike pretense intensely.

JOE: Oh do you.

> *(Pause. Then JOE comes up behind KEN and yanks his wig from his head.)*

KEN: Joe!

JOE: It's John, remember? John! No more pretense between old friends. This is *real intimacy.*

> *(KEN chases JOE, who is laughing, around the room.)*

KEN: Joe! John, please. *(Becoming increasingly hysterical.)* Give it back!

> *(With a cry of rage he leaps on JOE, knocking him to the floor and pinning him there. He tries to pry the wig from JOE's hands.)*

You're going to tear it, you're going to tear it!

> *(JOE throws the wig and KEN scrambles after it. Kneeling, he puts it on, gasping and trembling.)*

JOE: *(Watching him with disgust.)* Look at yourself. You're pathetic. *Pathetic.* What am I doing here with you?

(JOE leaves. KEN wrenches the wig from his head and throws it across the room.)

Scene Seven

(Lighting shift. Maybe the same night or maybe a few weeks later: 1967. KEN, in his pyjamas, is sitting on his bed reading the journal. On JOE's bed is a suitcase. JOE enters from outside.)

JOE: I told you not to wait up for me. What're you reading?

KEN: Your diary.

(JOE goes over to KEN and take it from him; reads a bit; laughs.)

JOE: Look, there you are.

KEN: I know. *(Pause.)* Kenneth H.

JOE: What?

KEN: My name. *(Pause.)* I finished packing for you. Look.

(He takes some socks from JOE's suitcase and holds them up.)

JOE: New socks.

KEN: I also went to see Dr. Ismay. I didn't have an appointment but he agreed to see me anyway. He prescribed some medication. Which I went immediately to purchase. And took some. I'm just beginning to feel the effects. It's … quite miraculous. I feel incredibly calm. At peace, almost.

JOE: Only a few months more. Then we'll be back in Tangier.

KEN: I can't wait.

JOE: Meanwhile there are signs of life beyond this hell-hole-in-the-wall. I'll find you a new home. Lots of room to roam around in. Lots of … space.

KEN: And where will you be while I'm roaming round and round my spacious new accommodations?

(JOE begins to undress.)

JOE: I don't know yet. Not here. *(Pause.)* I'll stop by every weekend to see you.

KEN: So it's gone from "I'll never leave you" to "I'll stop by on weekends."

JOE: *(Simply.)* I'm not responsible for you.

KEN: *(Quietly.)* You're right.

JOE: *(Caught off guard.)* I know I am.

KEN: *(Slowly.)* And I understand that.

JOE: Do you?

KEN: Yes, now.

JOE: Then I'm glad.

KEN: Don't pretend you care.

JOE: But I do care.

KEN: I'm going to prove to you, Joe, that I can be responsible for myself.

JOE: I hope you do.

> *(He removes his underwear and sits naked on the bed. KEN turns to him. Pause.)*

   Ken—

KEN: What?

JOE: *(After a pause.)* Never mind.

KEN: What is it?

JOE: *(Climbing under the covers.)* Nothing. Just turn out the light when you're ready to go to sleep. *(Pause.)* Leicester tomorrow. The prodigal son returns in triumph. I've become a cliché.

KEN: *(A whisper.)* How does it feel?

> *(Pause as JOE considers.)*

JOE: Good.

KEN: Why?

JOE: Revenge.

> *(Pause.)*

KEN: Revenge?

JOE: I know you understand. *(Pause.)* You're invited, you know. To Leicester—with me. D'you want to come?

KEN: *(Surprised.)* No.

JOE: You don't want to see *Sloane* with me one more time?

KEN: I've never visited your sister and her family before. They wouldn't know what to make of me, I'm sure.

JOE: You'd be with me. They wouldn't have to make anything of you. *(Pause.)* You'll be all right on your own, then?

KEN: I told you, Joe. I'm responsible for myself now.

JOE: Right. Thought I should ask.

KEN: No, you go. Enjoy your revenge.

JOE: I will.

> *(KEN reaches over to turn off the light. Blackout.)*

Scene Eight

> *(Spotlight on KEN, who sits in the chair by JOE's bed, gripping the hammer. JOE steps from the shadows and takes the hammer from him. He goes over to his bed where he is again obscured by shadows. There is the sound of a hammer penetrating flesh and skull. Nine blows. The gore flies, hitting the walls, hitting KEN. When it's over JOE drops the hammer at KEN's feet. KEN rises and addresses the audience.)*

KEN: *(As if resuming a rudely interrupted conversation.)* You see, I've envisioned all the ways it could be undertaken, this … ending we're having. And I decided it would have to end in comedy.

> *(JOE steps out of the shadows, his body glistening with blood. KEN begins to undress.)*

JOE: Comedy?

KEN: Yes. *Black* comedy. I *have* evolved, somewhat, somehow, through pain. Once I would've thought tragedy the only fitting conclusion to our grim fairy tale. But now—and don't think I expect *you* to understand this—I've been … humbled.

JOE: *(Staring contemplatively at his bed.)* Life does that to one. Death, too.

KEN: *(With palpable relief.)* You do understand.

JOE: I do.

> *(JOE comes up behind KEN, who is now stripped naked. JOE takes KEN's pyjamas, folds them neatly, and drapes them over the desk chair.)*

KEN: I have been humbled, wrenched from my high horse and trampled in the dirt beneath its hoofs … *hooves?* See? I haven't even mastered syntax and now I'm going to have to … What was I—?

JOE: You were being humbled.

KEN: Yes. I no longer feel superior to your … primitive methods of obtaining … physical release. I'm having such difficulty—!

JOE: Fucking?

KEN: Hhmmm?

JOE: Is that what you meant by "physical release"?

KEN: More than mere "fucking," J— Well. I mean desire! Passion! The fact that precedes all else. It doesn't matter what the object of that desire is: animal, vegetable, mineral ...

JOE: Visceral.

KEN: Desire's the fact. And we must use whatever methods are at our disposal, our humble human disposal, to ... fulfill, to ... reach, a point of ... completion ... consummation ... where nothing is showing seams ...

(They are sitting on the floor. JOE, behind KEN, feeds him the pills and juice, one by one, sip by sip. When they're gone:)

JOE: I suppose there's nothing left to ask you, except ... What do you miss most about being alive?

KEN: *(After a long pause.)* Cleaning. *(Pause.)* Why hasn't there ever been any comfort for me? *(Pause.)* Am I wrong to ask that? Is this what it's like for everyone? *(Pause.)* It can't be true. It must just be me. *(Pause. With some irony.)* That's a comforting thought.

JOE: You want to know what *I* think? I think this is all a nightmare. It's all obviously a horrible dream.

KEN: *(Staring at his wrists.)* J— ... Look! *(A flash of joy.)* We're free. No handcuffs or handbags hanging between us ... *(Followed by horror.)* I'm *free!* *(Shudders.)* Hold me!

(KEN closes his eyes and lays his head in JOE's lap. JOE reflexively clutches at KEN.)

JOE: Only I can't be dreaming it because I'm dead. And whenever whoever *is* dreaming it wakes up I'll be gone. I want to live.

(Looks at KEN for the first time during the scene and addresses the still, silent figure.)

Don't wake up.

(Tableau. Lights fade.)

Plays available from Blizzard Publishing

☐ *Amigo's Blue Guitar*, MacLeod, J.
$10.95 (pb) 0-921368-23-2

☐ *Beautiful Lake Winnipeg*, Hunter, M.
$10.95 (pb) 0-921368-10-0

☐ *Bordertown Café*, Rebar, K.
$10.95 (pb) 0-921368-08-9

☐ *Castrato*, Nelson, G.
$11.95 (pb) 0-921368-31-3

☐ *Chinese Man Said Goodbye, The*,
McManus, B.
$10.95 (pb) 0-921368-05-4

☐ *Collateral Damage*, Robinson, M.
$10.95 (pb) 0-921368-40-2

☐ *Come Good Rain*, Seremba, G.
$10.95 (pb) 0-921368-34-8

☐ *Darling Family, The: A Duet for Three*,
Griffiths, L.
$10.95 (pb) 0-921368-17-8

☐ *Democracy*, Murrell, J.
$10.95 (pb) 0-921368-28-3

☐ *Departures and Arrivals*, Shields, C.
$10.95 (pb) 0-921368-13-5

☐ *Exile*, Crail, A.
$10.95 (pb) 0-921368-12-7

☐ *Fire*, Ledoux, P. & Young, D.
$9.95 (pb) 0-929091-05-1

☐ *Footprints On the Moon*, Hunter, M.
$10.95 (pb) 0-921368-07-0

☐ *Gravel Run*, Massing, C.
$10.95 (pb) 0-921368-16-X

☐ *Invention of Poetry, The*, Quarrington, P.
$9.95 (pb) 0-929091-31-0

☐ *Live With It*, Moore, E.
$10.95 (pb) 0-921368-39-9

☐ *Mail Order Bride, The*, Clinton, R.
$10.95 (pb) 0-921368-09-7

☐ *Memories of You*, Lill, W.
$9.95 (pb) 0-929091-06-X

☐ *Midnight Madness*, Carley, D.
$9.95 (pb) 0-920197-88-4

☐ *Mirror Game*, Foon, D.
$10.95 (pb) 0-921368-24-0

☐ *Oldest Living, The*, Smith, P.
$5.95 (pb) 0-920999-02-6

☐ *Prairie Report*, Moher, F.
$10.95 (pb) 0-921368-15-1

☐ *refugees*, Rintoul, H.
$7.95 (pb) 0-921368-02-X

☐ *Sky*, Gault, C.
$10.95 (pb) 0-921368-06-2

☐ *Soft Eclipse, The*, Gault, C.
$10.95 (pb) 0-921368-14-3

☐ *Steel Kiss*, Fulford, R.
$10.95 (pb) 0-921368-19-4

☐ *Stephen & Mr. Wilde*, Bartley, J.
$10.95 (pb) 0-921368-36-4

☐ *Stillborn Lover, The*, Findley, T.
$15.95 (hc) 0-921368-33-X

☐ *Third Ascent, The*, Moher, F.
$10.95 (pb) 0-921368-04-6

☐ *Thirteen Hands*, Shields, C.
$11.95 (pb) 0-921368-30-5

☐ *Transit of Venus*, Hunter, M.
$10.95 (pb) 0-921368-29-1

☐ *Unidentified Human Remains and the
True Nature of Love*, Fraser, B.
$10.95 (pb) 0-921368-11-9

☐ *Wild Guys, The*, Wreggitt & Shaw
$10.95 (pb) 0-921368-37-2

☐ *Writing With Our Feet*, Carley, D.
$10.95 (pb) 0-921368-20-8

Anthologies and Theatre Studies

- *Adventures for (Big) Girls: Seven Radio Plays*, Jansen, A. (Ed.)
  $16.95 (pb) 0-921368-32-1

- *Airborne: Radio Plays by Women*, Jansen, A. (Ed.)
  $14.95 (pb) 0-921368-22-4

- *Dangerous Traditions: A Passe Muraille Anthology*, Rudakoff, J. (Ed.)
  $19.95 (pb) 0-921368-27-5

- *Endangered Species: Four Plays*, Hollingsworth, M.
  $10.95 (pb) 0-9693639-0-1

- *Instant Applause:*
  26 very short complete plays
  $19.95 (pb) 0-921368-38-0

- *Take Five: The Morningside Dramas*, Carley, D. (Ed.)
  $14.95 (pb) 0-921368-21-6

- *Dramatic Body, The: A Guide to Physical Characterization*, Jetsmark, T. (trans. P. Brask)
  $15.95 (pb) 0-921368-25-9

- *Hot Ice: Shakespeare in Moscow, A Director's Diary*, Sprung, G. (with R. Much)
  $15.95 (pb) 0-921368-18-6

- *Women on the Canadian Stage: The Legacy of Hrotsvit*, Much, R. (Ed.)
  $16.95 (pb) 0-921368-26-7

To Order:

BLIZZARD PUBLISHING
301 - 89 Princess St., Winnipeg, MB
CANADA R3B 1K6

Please send me the titles I have indicated:

Name: ....

Address: ....

City: .... State/Prov.: .... Code: ....

Please send cheque or money order; no cash or C.O.D.
Add $2.50 for shipping; or 50¢ per book for orders of more than five books.
Canadian residents add 7% GST. Allow three weeks for delivery.

- Free catalogues available on request.